MR. BLUE will provide you with a *memorable reading experience*—

"Sometimes a perfect little work of genius is laid like a flawless sapphire or turquoise in the palm of one's hand: and contemplating it the sensation of gratitude is experienced as of a happy debt contracted than can not be paid either to the creator or his benefaction. Myles Connolly has put us all in his debt by writing MR. BLUE which has the short actualities of a genuine biography—the tale of a Spy of God sent here briefly to witness against us and our immense and futile follies."

—CATHOLIC WORLD

"Mr. Connolly has infused into his book a radiant sincerity, a quality of rememorable reality. . . . Mr. Connolly has produced as fine and strange a fantasy as has got into print in a very long time."

—COMMONWEAL

"Strangely moving and poignantly beautiful."

—PROVIDENCE JOURNAL

MR. BLUE

by Myles Connolly

COMPLETE AND UNABRIDGED

IMAGE BOOKS

A Division of Doubleday & Company, Inc.
Garden City, New York

Image Books edition 1954
by special arrangement with The Macmillan Company

ISBN: 0-385-02866-0

To Agnes Bevington

You will come, in a page or two, upon the story of Mr. Blue, and I hope you will find it diverting, but there is a story of the story of Mr. Blue, a sort of mystery story that might also prove diverting and I will take the risk that all preface-writers take and tell it here.

Some twenty-six years ago when Mr. Blue first tip-toed into the world, the world was, I regret to say, very old. The mechanists and pragmatists ruled science and philosophy with an austerely authoritarian and withering hand. In religion, the rationalist theologians were boldly and coldly reducing the strangenesses and wonders of religious faith to logic. Wisdom had become little more than a rumor, and there was a new, dull faith that knowledge was the only end worthy of the pursuit of man.

The world was not only old, but old in an unhealthy way, for its antics were very much the antics of the aged striving to belie their age and show one and all they were really very young. Hysteria was mistaken for gayety, and howling was somehow supposed to be related to laughter and the joy of living

7

was believed, even by scientists and philosophers, curious to relate, best found in the nearest bar or bottle.

Now Mr. Blue was young and he believed ardently in the joy of living that is the possession of the pure in heart, and in the laughter that comes from innocence surprised, and he would have died rather than have accepted the idea that the glory of life could be weighed and measured and codified, and that the wonders of religious faith could be filed away in neat little categories by logic and reason. Mr. Blue was for the splendid mysteriousness and happy madness of ordinary life, for them even when they had to be paid for by suffering and sacrifice, or, perhaps I should say, for them especially when they had to be paid for by suffering and sacrifice.

Please don't misunderstand me. I am not intimating here I am altogether on Mr. Blue's side and that I completely subscribe to all of his points of view. I don't. I incline, for example, to believe in order more than Mr. Blue. I am thus a little more, though only a little more, on the side of the theologians. I also am more interested in the ponderables and thus may be said to be more, a very little more, on the side of the scientists. I also feel that Mr. Blue, like Thoreau, failed to make the deeply important distinction that what is sauce for the bachelor may not be sauce for the married man and father at all. But enough of my differences with Mr. Blue.

The happy young gentleman came, as I say, into

that dismally hysterical world, into that aged world pretending so unhealthily to youth, and what happened? Nothing. Nothing whatsoever. He did not raise a whisper. He was thoroughly unseen and as thoroughly unheard.

True, some of the reviewers read him, as a matter of routine. And with a few, a very, very few exceptions, they found him dull and false. The religious press, particularly, seemed to regard him as an imposter and a bore. A few people bought copies, attracted, I imagine, by the pretty jacket of blue with its gold stars. But in general Mr. Blue was profoundly ignored. The world he came into was in no mood for a man of his kind of youth and his kind of laughter. He should have died. He did, in a fashion. One year, he sold only seventy copies. Even I, for all my affection for Mr. Blue, had to admit that in a world of two thousands of millions of people, seventy was hardly a multitude.

Then, after the year of the seventy copies, after the year of the apparent death, an unusual thing happened. Sales of the book began to increase. One of that last guard of seventy, one of that last brave battalion must, in a burst of heroism, have told someone about Mr. Blue's madness, and that someone in turn told about his madness to someone else. And so, I feel sure, it began. Perhaps there was more than one who spoke out. I do not know. It could be that on the hundredth anniversary of Mr. Blue's birth some nice gentleman from Macmillan or Doubleday, most decorous in a tall hat and frock coat, will put up a little bronze plaque to that gallant one or two or three who were such believers in Mr. Blue after the doctors had retired and the embalmer was downstairs in the living room awaiting the corpse. If the nice gentleman should do so, I would like to suggest that he put on the plaque some such words as, "Victory Belongs To The Weak," or, perhaps better, "Victory Belongs To The Humble." (An English elm on Boston Common near the Bandstand—by all means near the Bandstand—might be a proper setting for the plaque.)

Now herein there lies the mystery that I mentioned in the beginning, not a great mystery but one of the small mysteries, one of the multitudinous small mysteries that so largely made up the glory of life for Mr. Blue. Why, through the years, did not Mr. Blue vanish and be forgotten as the critics foretold or inferred, and as his own early career seemed to indicate? Why did he not follow the journey into oblivion of the great best sellers of his time, follow as a meek and weak straggler in the dust of the march to extinction of the considered giants of his day? Why, after years in the great, cold silence, did he come to life and grow in vigor and popularity until on his silver anniversary he was making more friends here and abroad than he had in any year in the previous twenty-five?

Why? I do not know. Certainly, I had nothing to do with it. Could it be that there is something in Mr.

Blue's particular philosophy that is more acceptable in these recent years? Could it be that the world has grown younger? Wiser? Happier?

There are some slight, some very slight signs that this startling and unbelievable transformation might possibly be taking place. Recently I read in a book by one of the leading physicists of the world that a new principle has been added to the scientific method— the "principle of uncertainty." The deadly certitude of the mechanists of Mr. Blue's early days is apparently in fashion no more. The pragmatists, if my old eyes do not fail me, seem to have found pragmatism considerably unpragmatic. It further appears to me, if only vaguely, that Christians are not making so much of a secret of their joy as once they did. However, I have not, I must say, observed any great display of Christian laughter in private or public life. But then I have not been out and around in the world much lately.

It would be wonderful indeed if in the last quarter of a century it has happened that the world has become more alert to the deeply beautiful intangibles of everyday existence, and more aware of the strange and tender God who by His birth and life and death has given individual birth and life and death, no matter how obscure and drab and common, a radiant and prevailing glory and an everlasting importance.

It would be, as I say, wonderful if all this, or even a small part of it, were true. It would help to explain the mystery of Mr. Blue's revival and growing popu-

larity. I do not know. It could be. It could always be one of those incredible and impossible things that take place so often in the life of the spirit of man.
MYLES CONNOLLY, April, 1954

I give here briefly and roughly a few episodes from the latter years of J. Blue. Mr. Blue was an unique figure in American life. It is a pity his story is so little known. I hope this contribution will lead those who knew him better, especially in his earlier days, to add their bit to a fitting and useful monument to his memory.

Some years ago it was written of Mr. Blue:

It is impossible to be with him an hour without breathing a new wholesome air, charged with beauty. It is impossible to be with him and not catch the spectacular glory of the present moment. At the power of his presence, before the eloquence of his eyes, poverty, neglect, and such trifles become as nothing. One feels bathed in a brilliant and even tangible light, for it is the light he sees, and which, he would have us believe, is about us on our gallant journey toward death. All the scales of pettiness fall off the soul. The spirit stands up, clean, shining, valiant, in an unconscious effort to match his. But then he is gone, with his tears and laughter and his dazzling glory. "Come, come," his eyes say. "Behold the perilous road!" No one follows, I believe. And sometimes I wonder if he cares. "You will die, stifled with comfortability and normality, choked by small joys and small sorrows." Such is his warning as he goes. What can a man do with a fellow like that?

This passage caught the spirit of his life very well. But no writing could catch the splendor of his adventures. Let not the critical think that I have tried to do so in this book.

·I·

I had not heard from Blue for a year. He had written
me from England where he had gone on a pilgrim-
age to Tyburn and the places of Thomas More. He
had written something about generosity or humor.
I had written back, urging him to get a good job
with a reliable firm or he would end up in the poorhouse. "That will be glorious," he replied. "I have
long known the magnificent possibilities of living in
a poorhouse. I will become the troubadour of the
poorhouse."

I have not the slightest doubt he would have been,
in spite of his youth (he was not yet thirty), immensely happy in a poorhouse. He had no money.
When by accident he happened upon some he gave
it away. He worked here and there for his meals and
a place to sleep. He roamed eastern United States
and really did get abroad. The while he lived glori-
ously, and, withal, religiously. He impressed one as
a sort of gay, young and gallant monk without an
Order. Or perhaps his Order was life, and the world
his monastery. I suppose he deserved little credit for
his courage, his disdain of money and comfort, his

laughter, for all these qualities were as spontaneous in him as smugness and caution are in you or me. Yet, his life was his vocation. He created, wherever he went, a sense of the adventurousness and beauty of existence. He made people friendlier and drove not a few to generosity. And he inspired some young men I know to really noble ambitions. One or two of these ambitions will, I feel sure, be fulfilled.

I would have wagered with you that he would come back from England penniless and much wiser, that he would begin to see the folly of his haphazard life, that he would find himself some reputable office work and settle down to the normal, sensible existence of a good American citizen.

I was, accordingly, astonished when I discovered him on Park Avenue lolling in the tonneau of an unnamable foreign automobile, with a chauffeur and footman stiff-backed before him. The automobile was a magnificent creation, very much like a Hispano-Suiza cabriolet, in ebony with the most delicate of white enamel and silver trimmings. The chauffeur and footman matched, even to the silver, the decorative scheme of the car. Blue lay deep in gorgeous pillows which were massed against the dark upholstery. He looked for all the world like a child in its first fine robes in its first fine baby carriage. His eyes were bright. I could see from his lips he was singing, singing perhaps some flamboyant song of his own making.

The car had rolled by when Blue caught sight of

me. I was too astounded even to salute him. The car came up to the curb. Blue slid out to the sidewalk, kicking three blue-and-orange cushions to the street. They lay there, huge swollen flowers in the dirt. He looked like a college boy on a holiday.

"What do you think of it? It's my own idea," he broke out.

"What?"

"The automobile."

And this was his greeting after a year!

He had come over the road from Boston and hired, so far as I could gather, the entire Ambassador. Wouldn't I stop in for a bit to eat?

I stopped in for the bit which was served with candles in his own private rooms. He had a whole corps of waiters for the two of us and a major-domo to run the show.

"Well," he was laughing at me from a lounge in the drawing room afterwards, "what's your guess?"

"Crazy."

His eyes twinkled. "No. Not that."

"I give up."

"Behold a plutocrat. An uncle who made a fortune in Roumanian oil left me five million dollars."

Sure enough. Blue had become a millionaire, although I found out afterwards that his fortune was two million, and was left him by a cousin. He had made it in Australia where a great deal of it was in real estate and sheep holdings. Blue promptly turned every possible investment into cash which he kept on check in numerous banks. He had a little library case of these check books and was very proud of them. "I have more checking accounts than anyone alive," was his happy boast.

I believe he did. One day I counted sixty-three of these books on sixty-three different banks. It is remarkable what a man can do with money.

Believe me, Blue did some amazing things with his money. He bought three or four palatial houses and filled them full of run-down servants. He used only one of the houses but he always saw to it that the servants had a good time. He bought his favorite mansion from an old Boston aristocrat, bought it with all the furnishings. It was over-stuffed when he took it, crammed full of lumpy, useless furniture and atrocious pictures. Blue remedied all this by doubling everything. That is, if a room had ten chairs, he ordered twenty put into it. If a room had six pictures and two tables, he saw to it that there were twelve pictures and four tables. He carried out the former owner's designs to an amazing absurdity.

The pleasure of being around where so much money was thrown away drew me to Blue's company. At first, I remonstrated with him. For I had the old-fashioned idea that money is something you treasure or use to acquire more money. It had never occurred to me that money was a handy medium of exchange. Blue, with his usual intuitive wisdom, knew all this. He exchanged money for everything possible. He exchanged it with the poor for their delight. He exchanged it with the helpless for lighter hearts. I thought at one time he was setting a bad example for other plutocrats. But the fear was unfounded. Nobody imitated him.

I came upon him in his library, lying on the floor with his check books and a heap of marked papers around him. He was evidently in great glee. "I have spent just nine hundred thousand dollars in eight months," he announced, leaning back, his arms as stiff braces behind him. He was exultant. (I found out afterwards that he had spent somewhat over a million.) "And believe it or not," he continued, "I have a million left."

He built a little factory for the manufacture of toy balloons. Colored toy balloons were one of his great passions. He designed various shapes and color schemes, and had the balloons made accordingly. His favorites remained, however, the plain round balloons with the plain bright colors. He would go out into the hills with hundreds of these balloons, and, lying on his back on some high crest, set them off. He made up little ditties to sing with the launching of the balloons. I never have seen and never expect to see a happier man than Blue on his back on the green grass watching with enrapt bright eyes a gorgeous orange balloon fade in the hazy skies. Sometimes, when the wind was toward the gas house, he would attach a small bill, perhaps of fifty or a hundred dollars, to the balloons. This was a ritual that gave him great delight. On other days he would paint, in contrasting colors, rhyming couplets on the balloons and send these too off into the skies.

I suppose Blue had a purpose in all this business. He struck me sometimes as being suspiciously naïve. He had the boyishness of the true mystic. There were those who thought him crazy. Whether or not he had a purpose, he certainly succeeded in producing a very definite effect on me. I have always been extremely fond of money. There's no question about a man's best friend being his bank book. And yet, I must confess this madcap Blue put the stuff in a rather bad light, and made one feel that making it was a ridiculous and nonsensical business. I suppose it is a bit foolish to spend the few years one has here accumulating any commodity. But, then, a man wants comfort and the things money can buy. I told Blue this once, and he laughed until I felt uneasy. "My dear boy," he said to me, ten years his senior, "my dear boy, it makes no difference what you want or what you do."

"What do you mean?" I queried.

"What I said." And he laughed again.

I was in New York for a few months. When I returned to Boston, I made a call. McCarthy, his favorite butler, came to the door in his shirtsleeves. I missed the usual ornate uniform. I knew something was up. McCarthy told me.

Blue had given away the last of his money, sold all his effects, paid off all his help, and disappeared.

I had a devil of a time finding him.

A month or so later—autumn it was—I was tramping across Boston Common when, lo, before me, bareheaded, hands in his pockets, kicking up the leaves, is my friend Blue.

I took a delicious pleasure in trailing him as he slouched along. He had on a suit of clothes which was either very cheap or very expensive, a hempen effect. I discovered later that the suit was made by Mr. Blue himself out of the substance of three burlap bags. It struck me as being an excellent idea. I followed him up Beacon Hill a block. He took a couple of turns and stopped before a house that might have been owned by one of the Adamses, one of those flat naïve affairs with a white door and a shiny brass knocker. It turned out to be a former residence of the Episcopal Dean of St. Paul's and was now run as a decent lodging house by a large German woman. Before Prohibition it enjoyed an honest reputation even among the ancients who, unimportant though they are, still hold on to this citadel of Boston's glory. But since Prohibition—well, since Prohibition there are few of us whose reputations have not suffered.

Blue turned the door knob. I touched his arm. He looked casually around. He smiled, as if he had left me an hour before.

"This," he said, "is the only place in Boston for a man to live in."

I looked him over carefully. He was exceedingly thin and a bit haggard, though his eyes were as luminous as ever. I asked him about his lost grandeur, his money, his establishments. He looked at me with that childlike look of his, his eyes straight at you but out of focus by yards.

"Come up," he said.

I went up. His quarters were in the attic. The furnishings of the room consisted of one bed with straw sticking out of the mattress, one chair, and an oil stove which, I imagine, Blue used for cooking, though I could see no signs of food. Perhaps Blue didn't eat any more. I was quite willing to believe anything.

He motioned me most gracefully to the single seat. No courtier in a palace was ever more considerate of his king than Blue of me. After a while, he began to laugh again. He stood before me, six lean feet of him in his burlap bags, his arms folded, twinkled at me, grinned at me. And then:

"What's your guess this time?"

"Crazy again."

I said this, but I didn't mean it. He had many of the marks of insanity but somehow he gave you the impression that we were all crazy and he alone was sane. He seemed to have such a simple purpose in his life and succeeded so well in being very noble and very happy that one hesitated to judge him. After all, there are few things—except, perhaps, accumulating money and real estate and a little glory —that mean as much as being very noble and very happy. After a substantial bank account I can think of nothing quite as important as happiness. One has to give him some credit.

He laughed at my guess. I mentioned again the fortune he had thrown away. He held up his palms prohibitively, as if he didn't want the subject mentioned.

"Those millions were a trial set me by my Lady Poverty."

He bowed politely as if to stress the sincerity of his words. He changed the subject.

"Don't you love it here?"

I could not summon much enthusiasm. "It would be better wouldn't it if you could see the Gardens or the State House or the River?"

He was a little hurt. "Look!" he pointed toward a small skylight. "Didn't you notice this?"

I hadn't particularly.

He pulled his bed over until it was directly under the skylight. He threw himself hastily on it.

"Watch," he cried. "Watch." He looked up through the skylight.

I looked. It was nothing much, a bright square of blue sky with strings of cloud slipping across it.

"Isn't that glorious? At night I lie here and watch the stars fill the frame. One of these nights the moon will be there for me. I can think so quietly with my eyes on my own piece of sky.

"I was saying to myself last night how I didn't have any property, but I did own a piece of sky. It's odd how the window makes you think you are all alone with its frame of stars."

I mentioned how Hans Christian Andersen used to sleep in an attic with the stars similarly above him.

"Andersen would have made a beautiful Catholic," he said.

I could not see the point, so I held my peace. He began to talk, talk intensely, brilliantly, talk not as if he were talking to me but to some vast audience that hung on every word. He talked of life, the adventure of life, the loveliness of life. It is an old theme, but this lanky picturesque egotist touched it up with glory. The room grew dark in the dusk but his words lighted it. He filled the attic with his great courageous enthusiasm. What a small challenge death has for such a lad, I thought.

It was dark. He stopped suddenly. There was quiet for a few minutes. Then a ripple of soft laughter.

"Was I preaching?"

I did not answer. I waited a minute and then said:

"Yes, life is beautiful. What are you doing to pay for it?"

I could hardly see him in the dark. Then, after a while, his voice came, and I had never heard it so grave, so, almost, tragic.

"Please, please," it begged; "what can I do?"

I wanted to give him the old advice: go to his confessor. But any advice seemed so futile when given to Blue. Instead, I took my hat and slipped downstairs.

I felt he would like to be alone.

It was still dusk in the street. Some students in a theological school nearby were practicing hymns. Lights were spurting out, street lights, window lights. I thought of the boy of the balloons and the limousines. It occurred to me suddenly that perhaps I was wrong about his self-sufficiency and that he needed someone. I turned and went back.

I knocked on the narrow door that led into the attic. There came no answer. I slipped in. The room was black except where at the end, above a tall screen I had not noticed before, there was a faint uncertain yellow glow. I was mystified. I walked the length of the room and looked.

Behind the screen was a tall black cross mounted on a slight elevation. It was a brutal, bare cross. Before it, to one side, burned a candle. And on the floor, on his knees, his hands on the floor, his head almost on his hands, his hair barely out of reach of the smoky candle, knelt the erstwhile gay and gallant Blue. It was a striking picture, the black cross, the black figure, and the splotch of yellow candle.

I drew back into the darkness of the room and waited. Blue made no sign or stir.

I tiptoed downstairs again and went down to the side of the river. It was cool there, and clear, and immensely open.

I first met Blue under odd circumstances. John Stuart and I were having a glass of beer together not far from City Hall. John was with the *Sun* in those days and the talk touched, as it inevitably did, on Frank Munsey. We were talking of great failures, not the glorious failures you find in the research laboratories of the Rockefeller Institute, or in the literature departments of Universities, or in the planning rooms of organizations like the General Electric, not the fine failures who have dreamed dreams too immense for themselves—too immense often for any mortal—and missed, but the failures who are thrust into greatness by the gods and are too weak to make any use of their fortune or too stupid to know what it is all about. Munsey always represented an uninspired failure to me. It was as if someone had tried to pour a lake into a water bucket. Stuart suggested that the size of the bucket made, in an absolute view of things, no difference so long as the bucket was full. It is a way the scholastics have of explaining the varying degrees of happiness in heaven. John is a scholastic, and a brilliant one to boot. I was going to remark that New York wasn't heaven, not quite at any rate, when a voice at my side by the bar piped up:

"I know a gent who's so happy he's almost crazy."

Happiness wasn't the burden of the conversation; but in those days no one was interested in carrying the burden of a conversation. Our new comrade, a sturdy little man with coarse ruddy cheeks and bright black eyes, looked up at us over one of Al's excellent free ham-on-rye sandwiches. His name was Stevens, as I remember it. He was, it turned out in talk, the superintendent of the Tootsall Building, a new thirty-story structure on lower Broadway. It was he who first introduced me to Blue.

One day (so Stevens told us by the bar), a tall lad with dark intense eyes and an easy nonchalant smile came to his office to rent some space on the roof of the building. He wanted to live on the roof. He had a tent he could pitch there, he said. Stevens was baffled. No one was renting space on skyscraper roofs in those days, not for pitching tents at any rate. He thought him mad. But the lad insisted he was sensible and in earnest. He set forth the advantages of living on the top of a skyscraper: the air, the view, the solitude, the closeness to the heavens. He spoke vividly of his plans: how he could dream there on his back, how he would use the tent only on stormy nights, how delightful the music of the city would be, compressed by distance into a single note, how he could fly kites there and liberate balloons and set off Roman candles, how he could shout there to his heart's content and, even, pray there.

"The first thing I knew," grinned Stevens, "I was beginning to think of living on the roof myself. The boy with his spellbinding almost had me sold. But I remembered the wind from the Atlantic is a gale up there more often than not, and I thought of the fog that hangs on the tops, and I knew all elevators stopped at nine p.m., so I argued myself out of the coma. Think of climbing up thirty stories to bed!"

But the lad would not be dissuaded. Stevens had no way of setting a price on the location. He gathered that his visitor was anything but wealthy. Finally, he agreed to let him have freedom of the roof provided that he, in turn, would fill in on the elevators and polish brass when special polishing was needed.

"You'd think I'd handed him over the British Isles," said Stevens, "the way his eyes shone. 'How can I ever thank you?' he asked me. I told him to keep below the parapet up there or the wind would blow him into Ohio. 'That would be an odd journey,' he mumbled seriously. I looked at him sharply. 'None of this suicide stuff, now,' I warned. He laughed at me. 'Suicide? I should say not! I'm just beginning to live.'"

So Blue became a tenant of the roof of the Tootsall, thirty-story skyscraper, Broadway, New York City, New York.

He was a rare tenant, according to Stevens. He

gave up the tent for an enormous packing case that he found somewhere in the building. Blue could stand up in the case and walk around in it with ease. He painted it on the outside a half dozen different colors but not without some pretense at design. It seemed to be covered with figures, figures of gaily-garbed soldiers marching, all marching. The colors were brilliant and the effect arresting. The case looked like a glorified circus wagon. On top of it Blue had nailed a long broom handle as a flagstaff. From the flagstaff flew a white crudely-cut pennon with the bold word, painted in red: *Courage*. It flew there, day and night, high over most of New York.

"There are higher buildings than ours," Blue used to say to Stevens, "but we have it on them. Our building is a fort." To Blue, that building rising up into the skies above Manhattan, towering at the time over all but eight or ten other structures, with its painted box and pennon on the roof and its red word *Courage*, was a citadel standing for something or other. It stood, I suppose, for what Blue stood for. It did not discourage Blue to tell him that to the millions of human microcosms that crawled up and down at the foot of his skyscraper the building was a tall structure and nothing more. "Anything so glorious as this," he said one afternoon out on the roof, "anything pushing up so into stars and skies, anything subduing the sea and rivers and landscape as this does, must have a glorious significance." He waved a long arm toward the blue-black ocean creeping up New York Harbor, creeping up the East River and the Hudson River, he waved to the stretches of Long Island, to the cliffs of New Jersey, to the stone thickets of Manhattan thinning out westward into the hills and levels of New York State, spreading out westward over the world. "Must," he said, "must have a glorious significance."

Blue had a regulation hospital cot on which he slept. He pitched his cot in the southwest corner of the rooftop, close to the parapet facing the harbor. He slept in his packing case only on rainy nights. It was spring when he moved up so the weather was with him.

I was interested in Stevens' tale, as you may imagine. Stuart was a bit bored. He had seen too many eccentrics in his day. After the incident of the band, John folded his newspapers under his arm and left to catch a train for Douglaston. But the incident made me more interested than before. I could catch glimpses of a curious wisdom in this lad Blue. I stayed.

Blue, according to Stevens, was very fond of band music. He would follow a vigorous band the whole length of a parade, never tiring of the blaring of the brass, the thumping of the drums. He especially liked martial music. His idea of one of the greatest offerings of life was a rich, full band with plenty of brass and drum and plenty of supplementary fifes, marching in gorgeous uniform, marching with high military bearing, marching down a broad avenue or boulevard out of the distance, metal flashing, uniforms flashing, marching proudly, nobly, radiantly, and playing some magnificent bizarre fighting tune. "The thump of it, and the pound of it, and the ring of it, and the call and challenge and command of it, start my blood racing, start my feet lifting, start my eyes searching, my heart stirring. . . . Surely, no man can deny there are things worth fighting for, worth dying for, who hears militant music like this." So Blue said to me in a lyric moment in later years when I knew him. I think it was the spectacle of marching uniformed men quite as much as the sound of marching music that thrilled him. Blue had little interest in form but he was ever hungry for color. A beautiful pool or splash of color, formless, accidental, would hold him enthralled. A chart of the spectrum, a red tile roof against a blue sky, an orange chalk disk on a school blackboard, a yellow hat under green trees, a spread of paint samples, weather flags, railroad signal lights, any sudden display of color would fascinate him, sometimes hold him as intensely as a sunset pageant or the shifting canvases of the sea. The spectacle of a colorfully uniformed band with dazzling brass coming down through the great shafts of sunlight and shadow of a high-walled avenue would lift Blue to another level. And when the music burst out, when it came tumbling like a gorgeous cataract down the street,

Blue was happier than it is given most men to be on earth.

One day, Blue invited Stevens to a little party he was giving on the roof. The time set was eight o'clock. Stevens stayed in town that night so he could attend. Blue had told him it was to be a private and exclusive affair.

Stevens arrived a little after eight. It was a hazy night, dark toward the harbor, dusky toward the sunset. Blue met him at the door on the roof. He was all courtesy and graciousness. His duties as host rested gaily upon him. He led him to a bench, borrowed from an office for the occasion, set against the parapet facing downtown. The light, such of it as came from the raised elevator shafts, was bad, and Stevens was almost seated before he observed a fellow guest: Abraham Morgenthau. Abe ran the newsstand at the subway entrance on the corner. He was a fat undersized talkative good-hearted Jew of about thirty-five who was everlastingly puzzled and amused at Blue. They were devoted friends. When Abe's little boy Morris was in the hospital, after his fall from the fire escape, Blue used to sit with him all afternoon telling him stories. Morris didn't understand Blue or his stories, any more than his father did, but he liked Blue. Abe had no use for the tops of skyscrapers. It was only his affection that brought him there that night.

Abe and Stevens waited. They were the only guests. Blue was enthusiastic, rubbing his hands, talking. "This is going to be a great surprise," he explained to them.

"It was," said Stevens. "He disappeared through the door for about five minutes. When he came back he was arm in arm with one of the funniest things I ever saw in my life—a tall, cadaverous Negro, three or four inches taller than himself,—and Blue must have been six feet—dressed in all the shiny braid and buttons in Harlem. There wasn't much light but what there was sparkled on that fellow, magnified, as the pictures say, a million times. Abe was scared, I think. He moved around nervously. The tall Negro had a cornet slung by gilt cords across his epauletted shoulder and brocaded breast. Blue brought him over proudly. 'Friends,' he says, 'I want you to meet a great friend of mine, General Grant.' Then, he introduced us. He wasn't fooling, not Blue. He was fond of this fellow. They both were all smiles.

"General Grant drew back to the center of the roof. He pulled himself up as high as he could, and, believe me, it was some high. A strip of light from one of the shafts fell on him like a stage light. He lifted his cornet, tilted his head back, and began to play. . . ." Stevens looked up at me with an intense seriousness. "I tell you I never heard anything like it in my life. Abe and I weren't laughing. I don't know what he played but it got me. And he could play it, standing up there, swaying. . . . The music was so startling, the whole thing so different, that I figured there must be a law against it and we'd all be pinched. You should have heard that music from that tall Negro alone up there. Abe was shivering. I felt funny. . . ."

I can't duplicate Stevens' description. There wasn't much poetry in Stevens but he knew when anything moved him. And I can imagine how that lone cornetist on the top of a skyscraper at night sending his music vibrating up into space, up into the stars, moved him.

Blue withdrew into the shadows until the General had finished. Then he rushed out. "Glorious! Magnificent!" he was crying. He shook the General's hand. "I'm proud of you," he said.

And then came the high point of the evening. The door opened cautiously. Suddenly, there piled out of it a dozen Negroes of all sizes and shapes, all dressed like General Grant, and all with instruments, trombones, cornets, drums, cymbals, all grinning. Blue stepped out to meet them.

"Abe was groaning," said Stevens, "and I was afraid Blue was going to jump off the roof or pull something more nutty."

Blue, it appears, had picked up a few dollars somewhere and had confided his idea for a "top-of-the-world band concert" (as he called it) to his friend Grant. Grant played in a band that suited Blue's plans. The result was the concert.

According to Stevens, there never was such a concert. The Negroes were able bandsmen. Blue, they knew, was a friend of the General. And the night, the height, the stars, the twinkling dark in the distance, the yellow haze over uptown Broadway, the silence, made them outdo themselves. "The music blazed so," said Stevens, "that you could almost see it." Blue wanted wild militant music only—"maniacal music" Stevens called it—and he got it. It must have been overwhelming up there. I suppose none of the drab citizens who tramp lower Broadway at that time of night heard or suspected the magnificent tumult on the roof of the Tootsall Building.

It was a strange concert.

I was eager to find out more about Blue. Stevens, I said to myself, has some sort of vagrant on his roof, but he probably exaggerates his eccentricities for the sake of a good story.

"I gather from your tale that this fellow is crazy," I remarked, "but I don't believe he's the marvelous youth you make him out to be."

Stevens took up the challenge.

"Come on," he said.

We left Al's together. Stevens stopped for a minute to call up his wife in Flushing to tell her he would be late. There was a wrangle over the telephone. Everybody in the cigar shop could hear it. Everybody enjoyed it. Stevens came out of the booth unruffled. It must have been a daily ritual with him.

We reached the Tootsall Building in a few minutes. An elevator shot us up the shaft to the roof. We looked around for Blue. It was dusk. Finally, Stevens spied him lying out on his back, on top of his packing case, his hands clasped under his head. I could see dimly the gaudiness of the case and could make out the line of Blue's body on top with his white face tilted up.

He came down in a jump.

"This is great," he cried, taking Stevens by the hand. "I've been lonesome all evening."

Stevens introduced us. Blue was enthusiastic. "Don't you like it up here?" he asked, searching me in the dark with his shining eyes—eyes that were keener, I thought, than most people suspected.

I confessed I did. Stevens and he carried on a conversation together; that is, Blue did the talking with Stevens answering rhetorical questions now and then. Blue overflowed with ideas. He wanted the owner of the building to build cottages on the roof for the scrubwomen and janitors. He had a plan which involved flower and vegetable gardens and a small playground and what-not. All needed, he declared, was twenty-four-hour elevator service and he felt sure the owner would not object to that. "Why," exclaimed Blue, "look at the good he could do!"

Stevens grinned. He knew the owner better than Blue. "If he knew you were up here," he returned, "he'd kick you off to-morrow."

Blue was worried. "I didn't know that," he said.

So the time went by. The more I listened to Blue the more I liked him. I liked his looks, to begin with. Anybody would. But besides that there was a certain spectacular quality—one might call it a certain spectacular sanity—beneath all his ideas that was novel and stimulating to me. This boy, I said to myself, is no mere crack-brain, however improvident and impractical he may be.

After a while, Stevens went down. I was left alone with Blue. He elaborated further to me his plan for letting the poor live on the top of skyscrapers. With the proper walls and protection, he maintained, they would be more comfortable than in their slums. "And then," he declared, "think of the beautiful lives they would live up on these clean heights. Think of the customs they would build up, and the literature they would create. Can't you picture a group of laboring men gathered together out over some cornice after their day's work, gazing into the sunset, and making the tales and legends of a new race of people? Can't you imagine the women putting up their fragrantly clean washing in the lofty winds of a May morning? Can't you see the new games the children would play, the new gayety in their hearts? Poor people with these horizons! Poor people with the whole beautiful world beneath them! Poor people up here in the skies!"

I suppose there are a million practical difficulties, even admitting the consent of the owners. But Blue made me see the poor living up there with him so vividly that I almost believed it true. Blue always made me feel that he, whatever the difficulties, could make any of his dreams come true.

The minutes passed. . . . Night had smothered

the city, and the city gave up its protest in uncount-
able millions of bubbles and gasps of light. Below
was glittering Manhattan. The east was black. The
opaque hilly horizon of the west was razor-edged
against a last gleam of cold white light. Destroyers
rode the unbridged Hudson; ferries and small craft
flecked her with light. The East River lay her dark
secretive self, coddling her treasure, Blackwell's
Island, lay a cool, lamp-spotted, many-bridged
stream between the sprawling white conflagrations
of Brooklyn and Manhattan. It was terrifyingly beautiful up on the roof, four hundred feet above the
gaudy streets, four hundred feet up in the cool dark
silences, four hundred feet up nearer the stars. What
a freedom! One instinctively drew deeper breath.
One instinctively expanded in stature, in gesture, in
vision. The voice alone tended to grow small, as if
in reverence. There was little wind. The parapet was
breast high. I leaned over it slightly to see Broadway
below. I shuddered. Broadway was darker here. The
great fountain of light at Times Square that inun-
dated the uptown streets trickled away in these
lower caverns.

Blue leaped up on the parapet, lightly with the
aid of one hand. I shivered. He stood there smiling
against the dark nothingness of the sky. He was talking, gesticulating. Then, he laughed. He seemed
twice as tall as before. "Behold," he said with a wave
toward the harbor, turning as he waved, "the ocean,
Italy, Spain, England, Europe. And now behold," he

went on with another gesture, this time turning toward the west, "now behold the farmlands and the deserts, California, the Pacific, Japan, China, the Orient. . . ."

"What a view one has from here!"

Three or four stars popped out. One large one shone above the boy's head. He was superb.

"God is more intimate here," he addressed me from the parapet. "Don't you find Him so? This is height without desolation, isolation without emptiness. I ride into Infinitude on the top of Manhattan Island!"

He leaped down. "I'm so happy that you're here. I wanted to share my world with someone. It helps me to realize what a beautiful world I have."

He stood before me for a moment, watching me. Then he asked: "Are you a Christian?" I nodded. He said: "You're lucky. We're both lucky."

He put his hands into his trouser pockets and leaned backward, his face toward the heavens, now filling with stars.

"I think," he whispered half to himself, "my heart would break with all this immensity if I did not know that God Himself once stood beneath it, a young man, as small as I."

Then, he turned to me slowly.

"Did it ever occur to you that it was Christ Who humanized infinitude, so to speak? When God became man He made you and me and the rest of us pretty important people. He not only redeemed us. He saved us from the terrible burden of infinity."

Blue rather caught me off my guard. I might have admitted in him a light turn for philosophy. I did not expect any such high-sounding speculation as this. But he was passionately serious. His eyes were glowing in the dark. He threw his hands up toward the stars: "My hands, my feet, my poor little brain, my eyes, my ears, all matter more than the whole sweep of these constellations!" he burst out. "God Himself, the God to Whom this whole universe-specked display is as nothing, God Himself had hands like mine and feet like mine, and eyes, and brain, and ears! . . . ." He looked at me intently. "Without Christ we would be little more than bacteria breeding on a pebble in space, or glints of ideas in a whirling void of abstractions. Because of Him, I can stand here out under this cold immensity and know that my infinitesmal pulse-beats and acts and thoughts are of more importance than this whole show of a universe. Only for Him, I would be crushed beneath the weight of all these worlds. Only for Him, I would tumble dazed into the gaping chasms of space and time. Only for Him, I would be confounded before the awful fertility and intricacy of all life. Only for Him, I would be the merest of animalcules crawling on the merest of motes in a frigid Infinity." He turned away from me, turned toward the spread of night behind the parapet. "But behold," he said, his voice rising with exultancy, "behold! God wept and laughed and dined and wined and suffered and died even as you and I.

Blah!—for the immensity of space! Blah!—for those who would have me a microcosm in the meaningless tangle of an endless evolution! I'm no microcosm. I, too, am a Son of God!"

He finished his outburst with a great gesture to the stars.

It was a full minute before he turned to me.

He must have seen the amazement on my face.

"I'm sorry," he said. "It's a sort of declaration of independence I make up in these high places."

I told him it was curiously impressive. He smiled. "I'm afraid it was rather long. Five years from now I shall probably be able to say all that in two or three sentences. Ten years from now I shall probably be able to sum it up in a line." He looked at me for a moment. "And fifteen years from now I shall probably keep it all to myself."

He was amused by this last observation.

"Imagine," he declared, "imagine anyone with anything good to tell keeping it to himself!"

My head was in a whirl.

He had raised me to the clouds with his brilliant apostrophe. He had seemed like some lean dark-haired archangel. Then, suddenly he was laughing. . . .

Blue, I must confess, was too much for me. His exuberance and courage were overwhelming. Besides, the night was too beautiful, too beautiful up there in the freedom of heaven. The stars, the sky, the wind, the water and land strewn with their own stars, all had a freshness unknown to me before. I suppose it was Blue who with his magic gave them that. I had had too much for one night. . . .

I left him with his big gaudy packing case and its pennon crying *Courage* to the stars.

The elevators were not running. I walked down the stairs. There must be a thousand steps from that high roof to the street. Yet, I do not remember coming down. I remember reaching the street and feeling somehow that it was good to be down on the level of the world again. And I also remember bending back and looking up along the front of the towering building, looking up to where the distant top disappeared in the dark, expecting to see Blue. . . . It was madness, of course. But Blue made one believe almost anything was possible.

· III ·

I left New York on business shortly after my first
meeting with Blue. It was June before I saw him
again.

He was on his knees on the roof painting a giant
box kite he had made. He painted with energetic
delight. The roof was splashed and daubed with the
bright green paint. He was splashed and daubed
with it. I had to keep several strides from him or I
would have been similarly splashed and daubed. His
face was streaked with green and his smile never
looked merrier than it did through the paint.

"I am Spring," he laughed, "and I'm just starting
out to paint the world!"

It wasn't hard to picture Blue tipping sky-high vats
of green paint down the hills and over the plains of
the world. And how he would drench the world!

It was a brilliant afternoon with the roof like a
float in the vast blue heaven. There was a gusty light
wind chasing a half dozen white clouds northward
high overhead. Blue finished off the painting of his
kite with a series of extravagant brush strokes that
sprayed paint over the roof. He chuckled to himself

as he did it. He was having glorious fun. And this, I said to myself, this is the passionately religious lad, the tall dark prophet who stood against the stars one night weeks before. . . . I did not know Blue so well then.

Blue announced his intention of flying the kite. That was one temptation he could never resist, he explained—the immediate flying of a new kite. "Who knows what a new kite will do? It may show powers undreamed of, special powers given it by accidental twists, fourth dimensional twists, with which it may pull the earth off its orbit, lug it into the way of the sun and planets, set them crossing, colliding, crashing, blasting the whole universe to pieces. That would be a kite! . . ." While he talked he fastened the kite by a slender strong cord that he unrolled from a great wooden spool. "What a kite! The least this green dragon can do is to pull me off the roof, pull me up over the city, up over the Great Lakes . . . up over Canada . . . up over Alaska . . . up over the North Pole! . . ."

He was still chuckling, delighted with his fancies.

Meanwhile, he made the kite ready. He set it on top of his multicolored packing case. Then, giving himself plenty of free cord, he sprinted to the edge of the roof. I thought he would go over the parapet. But just as he reached the edge, the kite caught the wind and up it went in little spurts. The spool unwound madly as Blue fed the kite more freedom. He was still against the parapet. There came a lull in the kite's progress. Blue kept pulling in the cord and releasing it, pulling it in and releasing it, to force the kite upward. Suddenly, cramped for arm room, he jumped up to the top of the parapet. And there, leaning backward over the city, leaning with nothing holding him but the uncertain pull of the kite on a piece of string, with four hundred feet of frightful space beneath him, he began to sing! . . . .

I couldn't stand it. The sight of him made me dizzy. I sat down on the roof to consolidate myself, to convince myself that I, at least, was safe. I did not look up until I heard his footsteps behind me.

"You came mighty near getting your wish for travel," I mumbled.

He did not hear me. His eyes were on the kite, now little more than a speck over the city. His face was serious. "I made a mistake," he said slowly. He looped the cord twice around a pipe on the roof and, sitting down, settled himself against the side of the packing case. "Yes, I made a mistake. I should have painted that kite red or yellow. It would look much better against the blue sky."

It didn't make any difference to me what color the kite was, or, for that matter, what color any kite was. Besides, it was almost invisible. I said so.

"I know," he returned, "but think of all the people uptown who are looking at it. Think of them."

I could see no reason to think of the people uptown. I doubted, in addition, if anyone up there could see it either. But the afternoon was too beautiful for argument. I settled myself down alongside of Blue and relaxed.

He toyed with the kite string and whistled. Blue could not whistle. He could no more carry a tune than a bullfrog. He simply blew a shrill sound from pursed lips, sometimes loudly, very loudly, sometimes softly. His low notes on the intake of his breath were plaintive. His high notes were piercing. He would start bravely out on one tune, shift, unconsciously, to another, and end up in confusion. He knew I was following his efforts. After a while he turned to me. "I have no interest in time or key," he said. "Tones are what I like."

He was serious. I had to laugh: he sounded so much like a child saying, "Peppermints are what I like," or "Balloons are what I like." I have since noticed that people with an unusually strong love of color have most often little ear for music. Any taste they may possess is for obviously emotional, preferably sentimental, music. To them the world is visible music; to them, as to the poet, the stars are melodies and the sunset makes music in the sky. So it was, I believe, with Blue.

The sun wore down toward the horizon. Where the kite was I didn't know. I couldn't see it from my position. The cord seemed to be taut. Blue was in a garrulous mood. He was always loquacious, but usually he delivered himself more or less consistently on one general theme. But this afternoon, he hopped like a sparrow from one thing to another. I could not follow him. After a while I did not try.

He turned to me, for example, with: "Can you tell me what became of Saint Augustine's son?"

I told him I didn't know, didn't know, indeed, that Augustine had been married.

"He wasn't married but he had a son," said Blue. "Do you know what become of Saint Francis Borgia's children?"

I had to confess ignorance.

"And what about Blessed Thomas More's family?"

Again I was at a loss. I advanced the information that some distant descendants of the English martyr had been devoted sons and daughters of the Faith. That was all I knew. It seems that Blue had been reading about Saint Louis and his eleven children somewhere, and that led him off into speculation concerning the various husbands and fathers who were great saints. "It's odd," he said, "that nowadays there's no special appeal to sainthood for the heads of families. The idea seems to be that, after a man is married, little else than an ordinary good Christian life is expected of him. In the ripe wisdom of noble husbandhood should lie, it seems to me, rare seeds of sanctity. . . ."

"You mean," I said, "every husband is a sort of martyr." I couldn't resist the old joke: Blue was so serious.

But he didn't hear me. He was off in a characteristic appeal for a special society for husbands and fathers under the patronage of Saint Joseph. "Why," he exclaimed, "a knowledge of saints like Borgia or More or Louis—statesmen, soldiers, leaders—would be better than a thousand sermons! What giants those men were in the world as well as religion!" Then he added with a smile: "And what families they had!"

He wanted me to promise to write a booklet for the purpose of organizing such a society. I did not commit myself.

A little later he had another idea: the publishing of a de luxe edition of the New Testament. (Blue was that uncommon person: a reader of the New Testament). The edition would be printed in large type on beautiful paper and be magnificently bound and illustrated. "I would try to make it as beautiful as an edition of the writings of a French decadent or an Italian dilettante. I might even try to make it a bit exclusive. Certainly, I should have the first issue purchased by subscription only." His eyes were shining. "You know," he said, "I really believe that people then would read the New Testament. Indeed, I wouldn't be surprised if they discovered Christ. I'll wager a cult would spring up here in New York and other cities for the imitation of Christ. I can see the papers announcing the 'birth of Christianity' . . . .

"That was the cause of Christian Science," said Blue: "Mrs. Eddy happened to read the New Testament."

Then, without prelude of any sort, he asked me if I didn't believe one meal a day enough for any man!

"Note," he said, "how much clearer your mind is when you're hungry." Before I could even formulate an idea, he was arguing for the abolition of hats. Then, he wanted to know if I ever felt peculiar before electric storms. And so, on and on. I cannot remember even a small part of the thousand things he talked about. Some of them were worth remembering. Some of them were not.

Most of his remarks were concerned with religious aspects of life. This struck me as strange in this age and generation. One expected that this striking and vigorous lad would have other diversions. He was audacious, merry, healthy. He had, indeed, all of those buoyant and vivid qualities I had been told were alien to religious recollection and the pious life. Perhaps my conception of the religious man was wrong. Perhaps he is the happiest man. I do not know. But I do know that it was Blue's philosophy which kept him from getting along in the world.

His obvious failure to become somebody, to attain a place in the community was a source of constant regret to me. He would not practice even the most elementary economies that might have started him on his way to wealth. He would not, indeed, favor with special courtesy and thought those influential men who were in a position to help him. All he wanted was to be happy and to live out his philosophy as he saw it. Argument was useless.

He rarely listened to my exhortations and when he did it was with a quizzical face as if he did not understand my attitude. Yet, my attitude was in no way mysterious: it was the attitude of everybody everywhere. Blue, I'm afraid, was not marked out for success.

Dusk came as we sat there that afternoon, came with a light fog out of the east. The kite had disappeared. The cord lay slack across the parapet. Blue was not the least interested. He was telling me a story. He had been talking about art and artists. He had little use for the art that is kept in galleries and museums and the halls of the rich. He had little use for that kind of art, he said, even when it was put up in a public square. The art he liked was dynamic art, the art that changed skylines, the art that created beautiful customs, that inspired men and women to love one another, the art, in brief, that transformed lives. The art that would do that tomorrow, he maintained, was the art of the motion picture. "Once," he said, "the cathedral builders and the troubadours, interpreting truth, created a beauty that was as current as language and almost as essential as blood. Then came the printed word to spread confusion, to throw a twilight over the world in which men became little more than shadows chasing shadows. But now, we have a new art, luminous, vivid, simple, stirring, persuasive, direct, universal, illimitable—the animated picture. It can create a new people, gracious and graceful, sensitive, kindly, religious, a people discovering in beauty the happiest revelation of God. No art has ever had the fu-

ture the motion picture has. If it fails, no art shall
have had as great and lamentable a failure."

I did not subscribe to all Blue's enthusiasm for the
motion picture. I knew, whatever he said about art,
his weakness for pictures: he took more delight in
children's picture books than any child. I chided him
on his positiveness. He simply shrugged his shoulders. Then, he told me this story.

It was a story for a motion picture, he explained.
I shall reproduce it as best I can. I do not hope to
catch the magnificence of it as he told it, there up on
the roof with the fog settling aimlessly over us like a
thin white smoke in the increasing dusk. I shall
never, I know, have a story told me as vividly again.

The last known Christian had been put to death.
(So Blue began.) He had been found living in a
lower level of an abandoned mine in South Africa.
He was ferreted out and brought to trial. He had
professed Christ. There was no tumult or clamor. He
had been locked in a lethal chamber. The gas was
admitted. In a few minutes he was dead. He was
found lying forward on his face where he had fallen
from his knees.

The International Government of the World announced the capture and execution. "The work of a
thousand years is now at an end," it declared in its
exultant bulletin. The day of the announcement was
a day of great rejoicing all over the earth. The IGW
—as the International Government of the World was

known—declared a half holiday for all workers. Great effigies of Christ on the Cross were burned at all the sub-capitals of the world. While the crosses flamed, the multitudes paraded and sang. It was the first time in a century that singing had been allowed. The work of extermination was over.

It was a strange world that witnessed this day of jubilation. The peoples of the whole earth had become slaves of a few masters. They had been herded into vast industrial centers, great mountains of stone and steel, banding the round earth like mountain chains, rising like huge wens on the face of the globe. But these men and women were not ordinary slaves. They were creatures of the machinery of a mechanical life, inferiors of the machines they operated, subsidiary attachments to the monsters of a new age. The fantasy of the philosopher had come true: machines had become superior to men. Men were not mere automatons; they were minor automatons, servants of a mechanical state.

The masters of the IGW were the sons of the masters who had established the state. Their sires had done their work with brutal and consummate efficiency. All rebellious races had been exterminated. All people unsuited for slavery, primarily Latins and Celts, were segregated and slain. Only the stolid, unimaginative, automatic races, dominantly Nordic, were preserved.

The days of the ecstatic, passionate, beauty-loving, liberty-seeking peoples had, as was early predicted, come to a close. The sluggish, frigid races had survived.

The founders of the world state had prepared carefully for centuries. It was a long, difficult work to concentrate control of all fuel, food, arms, and transportation into the hands of six men. It was a chemist who, by a master stroke of strategy, finally perfected the consolidation. All agriculture and horticulture on earth were destroyed by a gas that obliterated a thousand square miles of forest in an hour. All fields, farmlands, gardens, woodlands from the great wheat areas of Russia to the forest expanses of South America were turned into a fine powder that lay like mist along the earth for days and then disappeared. When the work was complete the earth was as bare almost as it had been when the primeval glaciers withdrew their icy crust and first left the earth bare and bald beneath the sun. No fruit or flower or grain or vegetable showed itself. And none was allowed to show itself. The cultivation of any food growth was punishable by life imprisonment in the mines in the bowels of the earth. The cultivation of any decorative growth, flower or tree or vine, was punishable by death.

The few thousand inhabitants of the world who had not been corralled into the huge black industrial fortresses came across the dusty levels and valleys seeking admittance. They were counted, given numbers, and assigned residential vaults. At first, people stared at these sun-browned slaves from the fields.

They ill-matched the white faces of the vault-dwellers. But soon they lost their sunlight and became white as their fellows and as characterless as the numbers on their backs. No one had names. Individuals were known by numbers, and numbers only. There were no families. When children were born they were taken to be bred by the IGW in central vaults maintained for the purpose. If a child showed imagination or fire or spirit or brilliancy or any non-Nordic trait, he was destroyed. The multitudes, everybody except the masters and their large families and directing engineers, lived in steel chambers in enormous cabinets that were on the average a thousand feet high. These cabinets were like great filing cases. Each chamber was the same size as each other, was fitted with the same steel furniture, had the same bare walls. The chambers differed only in numbers.

No one wanted revolt. The lives the slaves lived were mechanical almost to unconsciousness. It was an existence that suited their racial type. But had some freak appeared, some heroic soul with a love of liberty, he would have been helpless. The master stroke of the chemist had made revolt unachievable. It was the perfect servile state: no one wanted revolt, and if anyone had wanted revolt it would have been impossible.

Perfect slavery was assured in this manner: the only food obtainable was liquid which was furnished through pipes, as was water, from a central reservoir.

This liquid was of two kinds: a dark fluid which had lubricating qualities, and a lighter fluid which had sustaining and fuelizing qualities. The formulæ for these two fluids were guarded with a secrecy that precluded even an attempt at discovery. The chemist who evolved the formulæ was killed immediately after final tests had proved their efficacy for the common weal. (A huge statue was forthwith erected to his memory.) The king of kings, that is the master of Masters, alone knew the formulæ. Anyone who made the least query regarding them was slain. The IGW forbade curiosity with the same rigor that it forbade laughter. There was little need for prohibition in either case.

When No. 862,337, say, arose at dawn he went to a metal sink riveted to the wall. Over the sink were three pipes. One was water, one was the dark fluid, one was the light fluid. Before washing he took a glass of the dark fluid; after washing he took a glass of the light fluid. These two glasses were sufficient to provide him with sustenance until noon. At noon, he took two more glasses. At night, two more glasses. And so on, day and night, until he died. The slaves, I imagine, considered it a well-balanced diet.

The two fluids were very much like the oil and gasoline that were once used in automobiles. The airplanes which furnished the only transportation for the IGW used these two liquids for lubrication and fuel. When a driver left in the morning he took the same food he gave his engine. They both worked in pretty much the same way. Each industrial center was provided with a towering tank which served as a filling station. Each early morning would find a flock of airplanes buzzing around the top of the tank like flies over a dead fish.

If any section of the IGW empire ever became the least stubborn, not to say rebellious, these antiquated and Christian weaknesses could be quickly cured by shutting off the liquid food supply from the central reservoir. The slaves would immediately be without fuel or lubricant. It was a simple system.

Now, it so happened, said Blue, after he had described the IGW to me, that like all mundane achievements the IGW had an imperfection. Even this kingdom of the Anti-Christ, perfect as it was, had a weak point. And so like all things mundane it came to an end.

The great capital of the IGW was SC No. 1, in what was once known as New York. Blue called it New York and I shall. It is easier to say, for one thing, and for another it (even such as it is) leaves a more Christian taste on the tongue. The weak point in the IGW was a small, thin-faced wiry man who lived in a vault in New York. His number was 2,757,311. But Blue called him White, for Christian reasons. White was one of the last of the sun-browned country dwellers to come in after all vegetative life on the earth had been destroyed. He had come with a strange group of people from one of the outermost places. The examiners at the gate had hesitated to let him enter. He had a light in his eyes and it was well known that no genuine IGW slaves had light in their eyes. They thought at first that he might have been a throw-back to some destroyed race, but he had the proper credentials. They watched him carefully. In a few months he began to look like his fellow slaves. But the resemblance was only on the surface, said Blue, for his brain was afire and his heart bled.

White proved to be a good slave. He kept step. He walked with head bowed. He made no human noise that might soften the metallic din of the center. Winter came and went. White was beyond suspicion. But with the coming of spring he cast surreptitious glances sunward. At night he would look out of the ventilator at the stars. On Restday afternoon, he would go over to the hills across the western river. His fellow slaves could not understand his trips. "Why should he go over there," they would say to themselves, "when he could sit all day in the dark in his vault and stare at the floor?" But that was the extent of their inquiry. Thought was too much of an effort for them. Their sluggish minds would return with their eyes to the floor.

White had a purpose in the hills. He liked the open and the sunlight, though none of his fellows would believe it. But he had his eye out for something. One warm afternoon he found it in a distant valley miles from men: a small patch of brown moist earth. He knelt down reverently by it, and made a sign of a cross on himself, touching his forehead and

57

breast and shoulders with the first two fingers of his right hand. After a long while on his knees, he arose and made a sign of a cross in the air over the plot, murmuring as he did so. Then, with a glance at the airplanes that hummed by high over head, he took a little sack quickly from his breast and sprinkled its contents over the moist earth.

"I shall bring God back to earth," White told the silences beyond the western river.

Then, he returned to Vault No. 2,757,311.

Spring grew into summer over the heaps of metal and flesh that were known as cities, over the bare rock and soil that was known as earth. The people in New York noticed that the air had become warmer, and that was all. Some of them scarcely noticed that. But White knew and noticed. And now and then he returned from his visits across the river with a light on his face that was increasingly hard to conceal.

Autumn came. The patch of moist brown earth was now white with wheat that rippled like water to the slightest wind. It was a small patch; no one had seen it on land; no one could see it from the air.

One Restday White visited his plot early. When he returned at dusk he carried with him a small package of thin white wafers. He had cut down his wheat, beaten some of it into flour, had mixed the flour with water, rolled the paste into flat strips, and had baked them quickly over a fire made out of the remaining wheat.

White was jubilant that night.

He spent most of his sleeping hours on his knees. But the next day was a solemn day for him. It was the day on which the IGW announced the capture and execution of the last known Christian.

White spent the half holiday on his knees in his vault.

All afternoon he could see in the streets far below him the steady stream of black-garbed slaves, marching in slow step like prisoners, endlessly marching, monotoning their dismal pæan of triumph. All afternoon the dark chant, varied only by silence or the endless shuffling of heavy feet, rose to his ears. And all afternoon he stayed on his knees. Now and then, he would look out and up to where above the black metal towers and roofs the sky still shone a lucent, unbesmirched blue.

Night came. White did not go to bed. He unpacked a box he had brought with him from the country. It held clothes, shoes, some tools. In the bottom of it, wrapped in an old coat, was a large case. He went over its contents carefully. There were some robes, a shiny cup, two small bottles, a book, a slab of stone, some miscellaneous small boxes and metal pieces. He went over each carefully. He filled one of the bottles with water. The other was already filled with a dark red liquid. Then, he packed everything back carefully in the case and waited.

The city was as still as if death had stolen in and possessed it. White sat patiently through the night hours. The sky had a strange pallor, he thought, and there was a strange weight to the silence of the city. He did not know whether it forbode good or evil.

Two hours before dawn, he took up his case and made his way to the street. The streets were deserted. Always they were deserted at this hour as the slaves slept. But in the deserted dark of this night there was an unaccountable expectancy. The great masses of metal towered blackly upward, massed themselves hugely upward, as if threatening the stars. White walked quickly, a solitary speck of motion along the floors of the caverns of the monstrous city.

He reached the base of one giant structure that surpassed all others by a thousand feet, a memorial tower to one of the first masters of the IGW. He slipped into the only elevator and went hissing upward to the roof, a half mile above the earth. He locked the elevator at the roof so that it could not be summoned. Then, he set himself quickly to work. He changed his garments. In a few minutes, despite the dim starlight, he was done.

"On top of that black tower of the devil in the kingdom of the Anti-Christ," said Blue, "after all those centuries of extermination, there stood a priest in amice and alb, maniple, chasuble, girdle and stole, heir in a noble line of Christ's servants, clad in their symbols of chastity, charity, honor and faith. The figure of Christ's cross lay on his back. The anointment of Christ was on his soul. Before him was his altar, his case topped with altar stone and missal and chalice. On it lay the corporal with the wafer he had made from the wheat he had grown. By it stood the two cruets of water and wine. He waited until first there was a streak of light across the east. Then he bowed down before his altar. *In nomine Patris, et Filii, et Spiritus sancti. Amen.* The Mass had begun. He was keeping his promise to bring God back to earth."

Blue's voice was quivering. It was dark with night and fog. We still sat out on the roof. What time it was I did not know.

"The last Christian," said Blue fervidly, "was a priest. Can you see that heroic figure in the twilight of the world saying Mass in the citadel of the Anti-Christ? Can you hear the *Christe eleison* as he cries it to the breaking skies of dawn? Can you catch the murmur of the *Credo* as the winds carry it to the ends of the earth? Can you see him turning with shining face as he gives his *Dominus vobiscum* to the empty cathedral of the morning?

"It was magnificent," exclaimed Blue as if he were telling of something he saw. "And the while he is making the sign of the cross over the wafer of bread, the powers of the Anti-Christ are gathering. He has been seen.

"An early plane spied him as he bent over his altar in the first streaks of light. The warning has awakened the city.

"Below grows a tumult of multitudes. The clangor

of the alarms and the rumble of moving people rise to the top of the tower. But the priest does not hear. His soul is on his Mass. The morbid slaves below awakening from their sluggish sleep are electrified by cries of 'a priest! a priest!'

"Millions who would not lift a hand to save a friend or give a sign of affection, these apathetic slaves of the Anti-Christ, are transformed by this discovery of the Mass. Stolid, stupid peoples, insensible even to pain, need—as ever—only the mention of the priest and the Mass to drive them into unimaginable fury.

"The mobs surge about the base of the tower. There is no access to the upper levels save by the lone elevator. Their blasphemies rise in raucous uproar. Their frenzy would hurl over the structure itself if it could. . . . The while the priest is reverently at his Mass.

"*Veni sanctificator omnipotens, æterne Deus.* 'Come Thou Who makest holy, almighty and eternal God. . . .' He is beseeching the blessing of the Holy Ghost."

The Mass goes on.

"The Master of the IGW has summoned the marshal of his soldiers. 'Stop the Mass immediately!' he commands.

"The marshal reports that planes are speeding to the tower. 'The top is too small for a landing. It is a difficult shot . . .' he is explaining.

"The Master is furious. 'Bomb the tower. Destroy it. Demolish it. *But stop the Mass!* . . .'

"His face was black," said Blue. "From his own tower he could see the silhouetted figure bending over his small altar. He tears his flesh in his rage.

"Two, three, four planes are circling above the tower. One drops a huge shell. It misses and goes hurtling down to the street. It crashes in the heart of the insane mob, annihilating a black square of them, shattering the steel walls, shaking the structures for a mile around. Another bomb falls. Another misses. And again, there are slaughter and destruction below. . . .

"But now the priest bows low over his altar. *Qui pridie quam pateretur.* . . . He begins the words of the consecration, the words that shall change the bread and wine of his altar into the Body and Blood of Jesus Christ.

"He approaches Christ's own words at the Last Supper.

"One plane is now low over the roof of the tower, so low that the crew can make out the figure of the Cross on the priest's chasuble. A bomb is made ready. . . .

"And now the priest comes to the words that shall bring Christ to earth again. His head almost touches his altar: *Hoc est enim corpus meum.* . . ."

Blue was whispering. I think he was shivering.

"The bomb did not drop. No. No. There was a moment of awful silence. Then, a burst of light beside which day itself is dusk. Then, a trumpet peal, a single trumpet peal that shook the universe. Then, the sun blew up like a bubble. The stars and planets vanished like sparks. The earth burst asunder. . . . And through this unspeakably luminous new day, through the vault of the sky ribbed with lightning came Christ as He had come after the Resurrection. It was the end of the world!"

Blue's last words were just barely audible.

"The Kingdom of the Anti-Christ disappeared like ashes in a whirlwind. And hastening up out of their tombs and resting places came the souls of the just, happy, hearty, wholesome, to greet their king."

Blue paused. Then he added:

"Father White who had been No. 2,757,311 found himself a hero even in heaven."

So, he ended his story.

There must have been five minutes of silence. My body was cramped from its single position. My clothes were soggy from the fog. Yet, I had not noticed these things before. Blue was waiting for me to say something. I did not know what to say. I held my peace.

"Don't you think that would make a good picture?" he asked me finally.

He was close beside me, but I could hardly see him in the fog. I told him I couldn't tell. I suggested his theology was wrong. Isn't the Church to endure to the end of time?

"But think of the possibilities! The scenes! The theme! Think of a picture of Christ and the end of the world!"

I had to be honest with him. I told him that it would make the sort of picture which would appeal to himself and the few others like him. Outside of that, I said, I doubted if it would have much success. "And anyway," I added, "don't worry. It is one of those pictures that will never be made."

We parted soon after that—I, to get some food and warmth on the street; Blue, so far as I could gather, to meditate further his strange dream of the end of the world.

His story was a great story as Blue told it. But I do not repeat it here because of that. I repeat it here because it gives a better insight into the mind of Blue than anything else I know.

On my next visit to the Tootsall Building Blue was gone.

I could not realize it at first. It seemed as if he must always be there like the roof and the sky above it. But Stevens had disappeared and the new super-intendent refused to let Blue stay. He was afraid, he said, "that Blue might disturb the neighbors." I could picture poor Blue on the top of a thirty-story sky-scraper in the business heart of New York disturbing the neighbors! At any rate, he was gone. Abe knew nothing about him. I could not find him.

I tried to find Stevens, too, then and since. I have always thought that he might furnish some valuable details of Blue's life in New York. But Stevens had vanished. It seems that he was an inventor. One night he was trying to blow up the main vault of the Mansard Bank which occupies the first two floors of the Tootsall Building when he was discovered by the bank watchman. He told the watchman he had invented a new explosive—nitroglycerine, he called it—which he was going to give to Uncle Sam. He was only trying it out in the bank. The watchman was interested. Stevens told him to wait while he went for more of his explosive for a better demonstration. Nobody has seen Stevens since.

It was almost a year later before I saw Blue again. That was the day on Park Avenue when he drove up in his ebony limousine with silver trimmings . . . on his way, so to speak, to the bare black cross of his room on Beacon Hill.

· V ·

There are people who say that no such person as
Blue ever existed. There are others who admit his
existence but maintain he was crazy. There is absolutely no question of Blue's existence. I knew him.
I have no documents, birth certificates and the like,
but I suppose I could find them. I have all his letters
to me and his one serious poem which he sent me
without comment. The poem is signed "J. Blue," and
I print it here.

VERSES

By J. Blue

Human love is blind—
But how strange the love must be
Of the good and gracious God
Who died for the like of me.
So herein let us have hope
That our squalor find disguise
In the splendor of His heart,
In the glory of His eyes. . . .

Blue would have been tickled by the thought of anyone denying his existence. There was never anyone more alive than Blue. To those who maintain he was crazy, I have nothing to say. He was a stranger to almost all I hold sane and yet I have never known a saner man in all my life. If carrying out the first principles of religion and natural wisdom to their (for him) most perfect completion is insanity, as would be held by many an honest fool and dishonest liberal, then Blue was insane. But do you admit such a definition of insanity? Blue believed in humility and he was humble. He believed that nothing mattered outside of saving one's soul and making others noble and amiable, and he tried to do these things with more determination and uncomplaining courage than your captain of industry ever dreamed of, or ever could dream of. He made sacrifices that none of the world's heroes make.

Blue was not insane. His principles—and his acts proceeded from his principles if ever a man's did— were as sound as the catechism. He was born a Catholic, but he had all that enthusiasm of discovery which heaven usually reserves for converts. His faith did not transform things: it made him see things. And what he saw made him exuberant with that enthusiasm so foolishly thought madness. Strange things happened to him. He invited them. His very character created them. This is not difficult to understand. Blue was glorious, and all sorts of glorious things attended him. His whole career is as obvious and reasonable as daylight—and as magnificent. I cannot explain further.

How he supported himself I do not know. Once, in a winter before he became rich, I found him shoveling snow. I know, also, that he did some backdoor begging. I suppose he thought this a penance of some sort, though I could never understand why. He was the happiest man in a kitchen you ever saw. He loved the homely smell of things. And the Swedes and Irish and colored folk of the well-stocked kitchens of Boston's Back Bay adored him. They would have given him their savings if he had asked. I can imagine these good souls and Blue: how beautifully they would get along together, how easily they would understand one another, how much laughter would be created among them. They must have wondered sometimes at their lanky visitor with his natural courtesy and princely gestures, his laughing face and solemn, strange eyes. They must have sensed, too, in some subtle, vague way that Blue was no romantic vagabond, though I doubt if they suspected that his life was an amiable rebellion against all that their masters and mistresses represented. He had taken, I wager, his own vows of poverty, his own resolutions for mortification. I cannot imagine to whom he could have made a vow of obedience unless it were to the Lord Himself. Doubtless, his manner of life without any obligation in obedience lost him many graces. He might have joined an Order

of some sort in time, though he seemed the man to
start a new Order himself.

Blue, like most talkative people, disliked writing
letters. He disliked writing of any sort. It has been
only after prolonged and somewhat unsatisfactory
effort that I have been able to collect the eleven letters of his I now have. He wrote five letters to me in
all, one from England, four from Boston and New
York. The other six letters were forwarded to me by
some of Blue's acquaintances who had read my ad-
vertisements and wished to coöperate in this work.
To these good men I now acknowledge my indebt-
edness. No one of them knew Blue very well, but
each of them was eager to help in any way he could.
It is not their fault that this tribute to Blue is as
unsatisfactory as it is. I hope after the publication of
this document that others will come forward, possibly even some who knew Blue in his early years,
and volunteer their aid to a more fitting memorial.

I shall not quote all the letters at length. They are
all rather brief and a few are almost entirely personal. It is interesting to note that Blue with all his
naturalness of speech and gesture is formal and a
little stiff in his writing. There are few of us who
do not grow a trifle in importance when we take a
pen in hand.

In one of his first letters to me Blue wrote a paragraph which reveals him more intimately than a
dozen pages of my manuscript. He had been telling

me how many of his best friends were derelicts, at the bottom of life. Then he writes:

"You cannot understand how hard it is for one to be practical who hopes for tenderness behind every face, how hard it is for one to be severe and profound who believes himself to be living a story that is glorious and true. Others can be impersonal, but not one who believes that he is on an eminently personal adventure. Others can be important, but not one who is so small that he wonders why anyone save the infinitely kind God should be good to him. Others can be sensible, but not one who knows in his heart how few things really matter. Others can be sober and restrained, but not one who is mad with the loveliness of life, and almost blind with its beauty. So others can live with wise men and important men, while I must always presume on those who are kind enough to forgive and weak enough to understand."

Later in this letter he says very beautifully:

"Life gives you pretty much what you give it. She gives beauty to those who try to add to her beauty. She gives happiness to those who share their happiness with her. She gives, even, love to those who love her. But these are very, very few. Almost all of us have a capacity for being loved. But few of us have a capacity for loving."

It is in the same letter he writes of a mutual friend

that he "had the old and admirable idea that a Christian should have Christian customs and manners, Christian poetry and pleasures, should live, indeed, in that fragrant and lovely flowering of the Christian life which is called Christian culture."

His second letter is extremely interesting—to me, at any rate. It is written on the stationery of the exclusive Hotel Ganymede. How he happened to be there he does not say. His handwriting is obviously excited. I had dropped him a note advising him to be more thrifty and urging him to take more thought for the future. He writes back:

"And even you preach caution to me! How I detest that word! How it has written its evil over our lives. Why, a man can't be spontaneously affectionate today without being suspected of weakness! We are advised to watch ourselves. We are counseled to keep our thoughts to ourselves. Silence, caution, reserve, are urged as prime virtues. Our fear of exuberancy, of ecstasy, of any genuine passion, is being stamped on our faces and our lives. We become a thin-lipped, close-eyed people. A thousand fine inheritances are being compressed into a single character—and what a thin weak putty that character is! Once, I am told, men put on their shields and banners such brave words as Love, Audacity, Faith. Today we have written across a million pages and placards and billboards our slogans: Self-considerateness, Thrift, Safety first. We have about as much hunger for loveliness as a turtle. And about as much capacity for intense and varied living as a cabbage."

Blue could be positive enough when he felt like it. At the end of the same letter he adds a quieter paragraph on the same theme:

"Conservative historians describe any man with a passion for greatness as a megalomaniac. Conservative citizens regard such a man with suspicion. 'Look at him,' they say to one another, 'the idiot! Why doesn't he settle down and establish himself in the community? Why is he forever restless, forever trying to get something beyond him? The man is crazy.' These conservatives are partly right. Play life safe, and you'll keep out of harm. Be careful, be cautious, and you'll never die on Saint Helena. Your failure is measured by your aspirations. Aspire not, and you cannot fail. Columbus died in chains. Joan of Arc was burned at the stake. Let us all live snugly—and life will soon be little more than a thick, gelatinous stream of comfortability and ignorance."

His third letter is curious. It is nothing but a scrap of wrapping paper with a half dozen lines scribbled across it. There is no salutation. At the bottom just above the ragged edge is the one word 'Blue.' Blue's letters are on a strange assortment of papers of all colors and sizes. His poem, for example, came to me printed out in blue pencil on the back of a paper napkin. Here are the lines from the wrapping paper:

"Men are terrified at suffering, at even the thought of suffering. Yet, through suffering only can one attain wisdom. Through suffering only can one attain the greatest understanding. And without suffering it is hard to attain the kingdom of heaven."

His fourth letter was a reply to a note I had written him in which I objected to his upbraiding the world because it suspected all glorious gestures and attitudes. The world, I said, believes most of its nonconformists are crazy and sometimes the world is right. He did not answer directly. He merely wrote:

"Most of us like to pose. And most of us when we pose are found out. And most of us, accordingly, suffer. Yet, there is something to be said for posing. All poses reveal imagination. Some reveal vanity, to be sure, and some reveal humility. Every poseur does not deserve the black name of hypocrite. We meet a man who is playing at being hero or saint. The man may be tired of himself. He may know in his heart that he is not so good or great as he might be. His pose is an attempt at nobility. We laugh at him. But we are laughing at ourselves. It is because most of us are such poseurs to ourselves that we so readily find a poseur out."

His last letter to me is a letter from the Blue who wanted a moving picture of the end of the world. "And what after the end of the world?" he asks. The paragraph with his answer is, I am sure, well worth appearance in print.

"When the day comes that the sky is emptied of stars, and the sun is black, and the distraught winds have only the void for their lament, I am sure that somewhere men will be merry together, somewhere good hearts will greet good hearts, and somewhere our dreams of unbroken love and good talk and laughter will have come true. This is a glorious Somewhere, and it is far nearer to us than the stars. There Our Lady talks of children to unknown mothers who taught their many children the love of her single Son. There Saint Joseph is a man among peasants. There Xavier is home from his wars, and there Suarez and Aquinas have their arguments out. There Thomas More swaps jests with the older Teresa, while the younger Teresa gathers her roses. There Saint George boasts of his conquest of the dragon, and mayhap the Good Thief listens, or mayhap he hears little Saint Francis singing his songs. It is a good place, this Somewhere. It has been called Paradise. It has been called the Tavern at the End of the World. And it has been called Home. It is only Catholicism that would ever allow the like of me to hope some day to be there."

Blue must have had many friends. No man as generous of himself as he could have been long without them. Yet, he seems to have had few intimates. Friendship was one of life's fine things to him, and yet he did not look upon it altogether as the rest of us do. Sometimes, I think, he was a friend out of charity. Once, I gathered from his conversation, he had been mistaken in a friend. But he looked back on the treachery of the man he loved more with kindness than with pity, and more with pity than with grief. "Friendship, at worst," he once said to me, "is an investment. Your friend, no matter how he may turn out in the end, is an addition to your life. He brings some things, and whatever his disloyalty, these things he cannot take away."

Once I met Blue riding around with an unimportant little snob who had inherited some money. He was an immediate and constant irritation to me.

He seemed to think he deserved some credit for having the money he did not earn. He was offensively good-mannered—a trait common in men who have a passion for dancing attention on women and who, usually, cannot boast a genuine man friend in the world. He was using Blue, I surmised, as an exhibit. I mentioned this to Blue. He laughed.

"What a Christian you are!" he exclaimed. I think he was a friend to the fellow out of kindness. "I suppose you consider the exhortation 'love your neighbor' a figure of speech. You would love only the lovable. Did you ever try to love someone who was mean, petty, shallow, selfish? Try it."

I told him I was willing to try to love a villain but that I could not arouse any affection for a mere annoyance, an irremediable nobody. "I think I could love a lion," I said, "but I doubt very much if I ever could love a mosquito."

He regarded me seriously. "You consider yourself too much," he returned. "You could love a great enemy. Any healthy man could. Men have boasted that they were to be slain by Cæsar. But one needs more than vanity to love a—a—what you call a mosquito."

He meant, I suppose, that I needed special graces in charity and fortitude. But the topic to me, being a poor Christian as Blue intimated, was distasteful. I let it drop.

Blue was, I happened to learn, particularly fond of two Jewish lads. He was forever extolling their virtues. "No one," he said to me once, "is more generous and more loyal than a loyal and generous Jew."

It is to these men that I am indebted for three of the Blue letters. One, Mr. John Stone,* sent me this interesting passage from one of Blue's letters to him on the motion picture. Mr. Stone had, I gather, contemplated investing some money in the film industry. He mentioned this to Blue. The following long paragraph is the result. That Blue's remarks have no concern with the motion picture as an investment is typical of his impractical method of viewing things. Blue could see anything—even the motion picture —in terms of eternity!

"No printed word shall wring the new masses as did the printed words in the past. They have not time for the printed word. The day when a pamphlet distributed at a street corner could start a revolution

* Roxbury, Massachusetts.

or a new religion is over. The printed word is too common to be any longer compelling, and too slow to be any longer dynamic. If you want to reach the masses you can reach them through pictures. These new children can be bent and molded as they sit in the dark enrapt before the magic of the mobile screen. There, in the dark, they can be lifted out of their daily servitude. There, they can be raised high above their stone-and-steel environment. There, they can be brought to the high places and shown the deeps beyond the hard horizon. There, they can be taught to be superior to the great magnificent monsters that are their creations. There, they can be taught to love this terrible new civilization, because there they can be taught to look upon it as their child, and not as their master. Here, then, is a mission for any agency. Here is a destiny for an art second to none in history. For it is given to the motion picture to save the soul of a civilization!"

There was one thing Blue could not view with Christian forbearance. That was bigotry. Any manifestation of bigotry against any color or creed would send the blood to his face. Mr. Casril Wein, the second of his Jewish friends* very kindly forwarded me this letter from Blue on bigotry. I quote one paragraph which is enough to indicate the intensity of his feeling on the subject.

* Roxbury, Massachusetts.

"There are natural excellencies which exist without especial support from heaven: amiability, for example, and generosity. And it seems that there are natural vices which beset man without any especial spiritual depravity or intervention of the devil: timidity, say, or querulousness. But as there are the supernatural virtues, so there are what one may call the supernatural vices. At least there are vices which cannot be traced to indigestion or anemia, or to misinformation or to ignorance. Meanness is one such vice; boredom, another. But at the head of the list is one of the most vicious of vices, and that is bigotry. The cruelty of that hatred of one's fellows which we label bigotry is so intense and so devastating that one, in quest of its cause, must pass beyond the ordinary depravity of the world and the flesh, and look for that cause in the devil."

To Mr. Wein I am also indebted for this defense of loquaciousness by Blue. Blue was talkative. It is only natural that he should defend himself. Besides he had an antipathy to silent men. They were silent, he maintained, because they had nothing to say. Silence to him was a mask of vacuity. He was constantly amused at the success of the ruse. All the greatest men of the world, he maintained, were talkers.

"It is the humble man who risks his dignity to speak up for what he loves. It is the courageous man who dares contradiction and the acrimony of argument to defend his beliefs. If one loves anything, truth, beauty, woman, life, one will speak out. Genuine love cannot endure silence. Genuine love breaks out into speech. And when it is great love, it breaks out into song. Talk helps to relieve us of the tiresome burden of ourselves. It helps some of us to find out what we think. It is essential for the happiest companionship. One of the minor pleasures of affection is in the voicing of it. If you love your friend, says the song, tell him so. Talk helps one to get rid of the surplus enthusiasm that often blurs our ideas. Talk, as the sage says, relieves the tension of grief by dividing it. Talk is one of man's privileges, and with a little care it may be one of his blessings. The successful conversationalist is not the epigram-maker, for sustained brilliance is blinding. The successful conversationalist says unusual things in a usual way. The successful conversationalist is not the man who does not think stupid things, but the man who does not say the stupid things he thinks. Silence is essential to every happy conversation. But not too much silence. Too much silence may mean boredom, or bewilderment. And it may mean scorn. For silence is an able weapon of pride."

There are two letters which are both rather heavy and rather long. Blue must have been in a pedantic mood—a rare mood for him—when he wrote them. One is sent in by Mr. Albert Considine.* Mr. Considine first met Blue, he says, at a hockey match. Ice

* New York City.

hockey was a game, Mr. Considine tells me, that had a tremendous attraction for Blue. The letter has, however, nothing to do with hockey. It has, among other things, a commentary on the neglect of laughter in history, and is shrewd for a man who read as little as Blue.

"People remember sorrow much longer than they remember laughter. It is easier to revive your sad hours than it is to revive your gay ones. It is too bad, with all the amiability in the world, that tears should be so facile, and laughter require so much effort. Literature is to be blamed. It has never coöperated with the gayer side of mankind. The biographer is to be blamed as well as the poet and novelist. The biographer devotes his pages usually to the serious thoughts and undertakings of his subject. His laughter, however much or little it may be, is rarely recreated. The biographer exaggerates the serious side of man to give him importance, for it has always been felt, peculiarly enough, that seriousness is a sign of importance. The biographer stresses a man's work so much that the reader is led to believe that the subject did little else. And yet all men loaf far more than they work. All great men especially. It is a misfortune that the seriousness of men lives after them while their gayety dies with them. There is great need of a new school of biographers. And there is, similarly, great need for a new school of historians. The history of the past, especially of the distant past, reads much like a long and sombre obituary. And yet, those men of other days were as gay and gayer than we. As with individuals so with peoples: their gayety dies with them but their seriousness goes on forever. Historians describe early peoples as especially severe, grey creatures moving stolidly through laughterless twilights. Yet, the presumption is that early peoples, especially the so-called primitive peoples, were immensely much happier and heartier than we. Primitive peoples as we find them in contemporary life are most always gay. The older a civilization, the more it approaches the glumness of stagnation. Capacity for laughter could well be employed as the index of the wisdom of a man or a civilization."

The other letter was written to Dr. Frederick W. O'Brien* on Blue's returning to him a copy of Thoreau's "Walden." It has to do with Thoreau, of whom Blue seems to have known quite a little. It commends Thoreau's meditation on the pages headed, "What I Lived For," and then goes on:

"Now and then, a writer with an imagination on fire gives to truth a brilliant and spectacular beauty that is at once arresting and audacious. Such men are rare. And it is well to notice that it is their imaginations which are on fire, not their minds. For truth lends itself no more to theatricalism than the moun-

* Boston, Massachusetts.

tains, despite the psalm, lend themselves to dancing. Particularly grotesque Chinese lanterns seen across the lawn of a summer's night may appear arresting and audacious. But they are only Chinese lanterns. They decorate and beguile. They distract attention from the modest stars. But the stars are steadfast. They are mighty masses stabbing darkness with tiny dagger-points. To the searcher for sensationalism, they may be monotonous. But they move the thoughtful man to profound speculation and they make him humble. Modern ideas, with all the flash and sudden attractiveness of novelty, are Chinese lanterns. Truths are like the stars."

We are indebted to Mrs. John Murphy of Ruggles Street, Roxbury, Massachusetts, for this last letter.*

Mrs. Murphy runs a lodging house for "men from the yard." These are, I understand, men who work for the railroad nearby. Recently when Mrs. Murphy was "doing" the lodger's room she came across a biographical note I had written on Blue. "I knew him in a jiffy," she says. "He was with me for a few months after the war. A brave smiling lad. I thought he had the consumption. He was the kind. But his health was of the best."

Such was her picture of him.

Blue puzzled Mrs. Murphy. She judged him one

* Anyone who possesses further information of Blue of any sort will do a great kindness to Blue's friends by communicating with me.   M. C.

of those boys who always mean well but who, as she put it, never pay the rent. Mrs. Murphy is a trifle hard. Anyone might be after thirty years in a lodging house. She's a big round woman whose shrewd eyes belie the heartiness of herself.

"I spoke to him one day," she says, "how the rent was due. Oh, but he had a smiling way with him. It would melt the heart of a wheelbarrow. 'I forgot, Mrs. Murphy,' he says. 'I forgot. Honest. I asked my mother this morning for it.'

"Sure enough, he had the rent next day. He wanted to pay me double. 'Let's be good friends,' he says. 'It's black, bad business this money. Do you see how it comes between us?'"

Where Blue obtained the rent Mrs. Murphy never did discover.

"His mother had been dead twelve years or more, he told me once," explained Mrs. Murphy. "Perhaps his asking his mother was a joke of his. He was always a-joking. Once big Jim Dineen, a fine strong good-living man, hit O'Brien and O'Brien drunk. Blue picked up O'Brien, picked him up the good-for-nothin' like you would a child. 'Poor Dineen,' he says to O'Brien, 'poor Dineen, but I feel sorry for him.' And the rest of us feeling sorry for O'Brien.

"A strange lad he was, indeed, a strange lad."

Blue left Mrs. Murphy's establishment abruptly. That is, he went out one day and no one heard from him thereafter. "His rent was paid up and beyond," says Mrs. Murphy. "And the things he left were of no use at all. I couldn't give them even to the Salvation Army much less to the Sisters. A shirt, a hair brush, and a pair of socks. He never had much, poor fellow, but he always looked well. Wholesome, I mean, and company-like. I think it was how we used to look at his face and not at the rest of him."

But one thing he left which Mrs. Murphy kept, bless her. That was a long letter, typewritten and addressed to "My Good Dear Mother." I can picture Blue walking in to a public stenographer with his manuscript and asking her to typewrite it. And I can picture the stenographer as she made the copy. Mrs. Murphy, had she a little more imagination, could have discovered in the letter who it was who paid Blue's rent.

I must confess I liked the letter. I find a quality in it that wins me. Blue, properly directed, could have made some money out of his talent. I think he could have run a successful column on a daily newspaper. He had the human touch which could have been very fruitfully capitalized.

The letter goes:

"My good dear Mother,

"I have never liked any painting or statue of you I have ever seen. It is not that these representations disappoint me. That would be natural when I expect so much. It is that they touch me in no way at all as you have touched me yourself. I have no clear conception of you. Yet you are more real to me than the people around me. Oh, much more real than they. A thousand times, a thousand more real than they. Sometimes, it is true, my imagination supplies me with brief fancies of you. But they have no permanence. I do not keep them for my prayers. Yet, even these brief fancies are unlike any representation of you I have ever seen. Sometimes I have a quick picture of you as a mother with your face lined and worn with sorrow, and your hair gray. You are a little woman, bowed, but your eyes are full and clear with understanding. I suppose the theologians would object to such a representation of you. Many little mothers like this have I seen and I cannot tell you how my heart has been hurt for them. They, too, have come back from their Calvary, poor creatures, neglected and mute, paying the price of great love. I know that you, Mother, regardless of the theologians, will understand this picture of mine of you. You know these mothers who love you so. You are the Mother of them all.

"Then, I have another glimpse of you. You are a young mother, robust, active, with smiling eyes. I think Hilary Pepler has this picture in his verses:

"Our Lady was a Milkmaid,
    a peasant girl, and poor,
she whom Almighty God obeyed
    would scrub the dairy floor.

Our Lady well could merrimake
    and sing sweet songs to Him,

of butter, cheese, and curdle cake,
of how to milk and skim.

"I am sure you like Pepler's various verses about you. I wish I could write as well as he can. There would, then, be no need of this letter. But this quick picture of you as a young mother, which I have now and then, is extremely vivid. The main quality of it is your activity. You do not sit drearily. You do not move sanctimoniously about. There is a certain health and almost exuberance to your actions. I expect you to come right up and speak to me.

"You know John Mickel who has the candy shop on the corner. John claims he saw you one night. The people say that John is queer. Maybe. I know he used to limp a little before he met you and he doesn't limp now. I know, too, that you've come to many people. And it's always struck me as especially appropriate that your most important visits were to humble, common people. You might very well have come to John. John, you know, doesn't talk much about it. The story is in his eyes, though. Once, he told me how it was. He had been over to see his sister who was ill. On the way home, you came up to him. 'Hello, John,' you said. He felt absolutely natural with you. I can imagine that is the way you would come to people. You would call them by their first names. John is a good man. I think he's a saint. But you know more about that than I do. And if you really did visit John, you have a very good reason for it.

"All of this is apart from the purpose of this letter. I simply am telling you that I have no definite picture of you as I write to you. But, Mother, you are so real that if you withdrew your support I think I would actually fall down on the floor here like a man in a faint. Dear Mother, how have you endured me all these years! Only for you, I would have long been lost. For you it is who took me and led me out of strange ways and darknesses years ago. You it is who takes me by the hand now day by day. Only you would not grow tired of the like of me—of anyone so sinful, ungrateful, selfish. I'm afraid, Mother, of Your Son. I should be afraid of Him. I would not dare to lift my head were it not for you. For it is you who stand between me and His terrible justice.

"You see I cannot make myself clear to you. But I know you know I am not trying to be humble. The thought of my sins smites me down so that if there were not you I think I would fall into despair. And when I try to reason why you should continue to protect me I end in confusion. I can only throw myself on your love. I can only kneel and cry out: 'I don't deserve anything. Not even the greeting of a stranger. But, Mother, without you what am I going to do?'

"This is mad, isn't it? This is unreasonable. But I am helpless in my weakness. I, cowardly, feebly, selfishly, give the weight of my sins to you.

"The other day, Mother, I was thinking of what people would say when I'm dead.

"So, I thought I would leave them a line for my grave. That is, if I have a grave. I don't care one way or another. But I do wish someone would write these lines about me somewhere:

'Never was there a worse sinner,
And never was God kinder to one.'

"Mother, it's true. You know how true it is. You are the only explanation of God's kindness to me."

So Blue's letter ends. It is typical of Blue—begins by accident and ends up in the air. But I think it makes good reading. You see what I mean about Blue having the human touch that could be capitalized. They say humor sells best nowadays. But I really think that Blue's sincerity, under astute management, could have been made to pay dividends. You meet plenty of witty men but very few sincere ones. I am sure I have an idea here.

Mrs. Murphy does not agree with me. She knows men, she says, and if ever there was a useless one, it was Blue. She is still wondering how on earth he ever paid the rent.

Here, then, before me are these eleven letters, a motley queer eleven, the letters of an unusual lad. I knew Blue's faults as well as any man: his improvidence, his erraticism, his impracticability. I mourn that he did not put his mind to business. He might have left us a great legacy of commercial achievement, a noted name in the history of the practical progress of the world. Instead, he has left us only these ragged letters, such as they are, and the memory of his strange self.

We were tramping out in the Newtons, out around the twin reservoirs which they call lakes. Dusk was sifting out of Boston and giving the massed trees—of which there are plenty in Newton—that stealth and secrecy which is their pretense at night. Boston College, with its solid Gothic tower, stood black against the last smoking flame of the November sunset. We were down in the dark. But no one could mind the dark, even of November, with the Gothic that dominated the hill. Blue caught his breath at the magnificent silhouette.

"That gives me courage," he said, with his face up toward the hill crest. "Of late, I have been melancholy with autumn—a sign of adolescence or old age. But I couldn't be melancholy with that above me. Not that I care for the Gothic, but for what it represents. Sunsets may flare, and the blackness of hades eclipse the earth, but that will endure."

"An earthquake could toss it into the lakes," I objected.

"And so could the cataclysm at the end of the world. And so could a madman with dynamite. But where that stands there will always be something, though no stone is left upon a stone."

Blue is a mystic, and mystics while they appear crystal-clear are sometimes difficult to understand. He saw my shrugged shoulders.

"No great battle for a great cause can ever be forgotten. That up there is no mere group of college buildings; that up there is a battlefield, a sanctuary; that up there is a hearth and home for the Lost Cause that is never lost, the citadel of a strength that shall outlast the hill and rocks it stands upon.

"A great desolation grows about us but up there is the warmth of a fireside and the loveliness of a garden. There are shrines for the devout, but up there is a shrine for those who are going to war, for those who will see the shivering void beyond the rim of faith. Once heroes built fortresses against the Mongol and the Saracen; now they must build fortresses against the whole world. Once they fought with spear and pikestaff against hordes of riding men. Today they must fight against pride and indifference and knowledge, against the agnosticism that like a poison gas decomposes the minds of the earth.

"I tell you I know what I am talking about. Once they—the believers, the students, the scholars, the soldiers, the saints—could fight heresies and heretics. Today they have to fight a state of mind. One might as well fight a plague with a bow and arrow. . . ."

Perhaps, I did not get Blue's conversation correctly. I think, however, one can discover some of his meaning in what I try thus crudely to quote. I, who have fooled somewhat with the printed word, suggested books and magazines and newspapers as weapons.

There was the nearest thing to scorn in Blue's reply that I have ever heard from him.

"The printed word has ruined the intellect. It has given fools and fiends the same power as wise men and saints. It has made a jumble of the mind, a burlesque of reason. No one any longer knows how to think clearly and cogently to a finish. . . . Remember Christ wrote nothing except those mysterious words on the sand. One gesture of Saint Francis of Assisi is greater than a tome. Napoleon knew this. When he wanted to change the map and mind of Europe he did not begin by writing books. The astute man contemplates writing only when his useful days are over.

"You are interested in preaching and teaching. I'm not. An amiable good life does more than all the religious newspapers printed. . . ."

"But you're preaching just now," I inserted. "But not teaching. I don't believe you. We have the printed word. Everybody employs it. We must. There is no way out except by rhetoric. . . ."

He smiled. "I suppose I was preaching. I like to hear the sound of my voice—especially in a fragrant stillness like this. I really know little about the whole business. I suppose the truth is that the printed word was good for something once but it isn't any more."

He was laughing again. "If *you're* so interested in reformation," he went on, "why don't you start a school of religious art here in the United States? All heaven knows we need it. Hire a floor in the Woolworth Building or in the Bush Terminal Building, in some majestic structure built in the spirit of the age. Round up a dozen full-blooded huskies—lads with courage as well as sensitiveness. Share your vision with them until they are on fire with a pentecostal ardor. Then, put them to work under a great banner: *We Ourselves.*

"I am speaking figuratively, of course. You can't make artists merely by lecturing them. But something should be done. Youth is crying for fertilization.

"There must be young men today who are manfully and spiritedly religious,—industrious, amiable, exuberant lads. Find them. Dynamize them! Tell them to be loyal sons of their age as well as their religion. How else can they be great in art?"

Blue was vigorous. He was intense—almost oratorical—in his speech.

"The poet saw Christ on the Thames. We might find Him on the Hudson or the Charles. We might meet our Lady by the lakes here—as once did a boy at Guadalupe and a girl at Lourdes. The sight would be our reward for being loyal to our Faith, our life and age. So, too, comes the vision to the artist!

"Tell your artists to immerse themselves in the fresh waters of the Faith and come up, vibrant, clean, alert to the world around them. Then, they are ready to design or paint, to carve or write or compose, ready to interpret eternal truth in living terms, eternal beauty in vivid images of the present. Great men dominate their age with their own art. But their art, when great, is almost as much of their age as it is of themselves. They do not achieve greatness by fleeing the present, or by bowing down in timid affection before the past. They do not try to cast their minds and imaginations into Classic molds or Gothic molds or Renaissance molds. No. They take contemporary life avidly into their arms . . . and out of the union is born their art."

Blue made a gesture up toward the Gothic that dominated the hill.

"Gothic was an interpretation of the Faith in medieval Europe. What architecture have we now that is an interpretation of the Faith in the modern world? None. Saint Patrick's Cathedral is an anachronism on Fifth Avenue. The Cathedral of Saint John the Divine rises a huge and blundering anomaly. That they surpass the monstrosities of American ecclesiastical art does not justify them. They have a beauty, it is true, imitative and borrowed though it be, that towers above the broken spirit of church structures that are little more than compromises with Mammon. They *aspire*, at any rate. But why these ancient forms? Gothic is not an article of faith.

"Is this the vision that is to vivify contemporary American life? Has the final architectural expression of the religious spirit been made? Was the last stone in sublime church architecture laid seven hundred years ago? Have we no greatness to contribute? Has all steam and oil and electricity, all this building and expansion and industry, all this vision and invention and labor, all this creation and munificence, brought not one small thing to the House of God? I cannot believe it. (I speak only of Church architecture. The other arts are beyond comment.) Something is wrong with your artists. It is cowardice to blame the age. Perhaps it is their art. Perhaps it is the dryness and dullness of their souls. . . ."

On and on he went. We circled the lakes twice. I was hungry but I hated to interrupt. I disagreed entirely with him on Gothic. But, I did not want to argue. Blue was usually wrong when he talked a great deal—and who isn't?—yet he always managed to say some things worth remembering. He gave me several ideas: that one about the artists, for example. Catholicism in the United States cannot be very deep or ardent or it would have flowered out into some sort of modern painting or architecture. And another idea he gave me is worth thinking over: the idea that it is growing harder and harder to keep the Faith. As Blue said: "I tremble when I think of the boys a century from now." Scientific agnosticism is here for a long stay, he maintained, because it is not a philosophy but a somewhat vainglorious state of mind. It is hard to oppose it with reason and argument. The only thing to oppose it with—as he pointed out—is another state of mind. And that, I suppose, is where great lives and good art come in.

I have reproduced too much of the haphazard conversation of Blue, but I have done it with a purpose: to show that Blue, while he may not have sat long hours over books, was nevertheless somewhat of a thinker on his own account; not a profound thinker, to be sure, but keen and independent.

As to books, he once said: "Books are for people who cannot make up their minds or have no minds to make up." He regarded most reading as a form of parasitism.

We took a street car at Beacon Street and ended up in an old oyster house downtown. It was the oldest in Boston, I believe. The food was a very reasonable compromise between quality and price, and I enjoyed it. Blue did not eat much. He finished half a clam chowder, nibbled a few crackers, and passed up the rest. He was extremely serious, as he had been all evening. Such sustained seriousness was rare in Blue. I said to him:

"Why should you be serious? You are the happiest man in the world."

He looked at me with his head tilted back a bit in the manner some school teachers assume toward their pupils.

"It is because I have been so happy that I am so serious."

I thought that over for a minute or two, but got nowhere with it.

"Sort of action and reaction, you mean."

"No. I don't think your queer pendulum rule applies to intelligent happiness. I have been so happy all my life that I am afraid when I think of it. I suffered a bit when I was very young, but that little torture could hardly have purchased all the splendor since. I've been the happiest man in the world. I believe I still am—if I dared let myself think about it."

This was a little new to me: a man worried because he was so happy.

"Heaven has given you your happiness: your health, your courage, your gayety, your philosophy. Accept them. Rejoice."

Again he looked at me. I tempted him with a red-and-white bit of solid, dripping lobster meat. He did not even see the extended fork.

"Heaven has given me many things and I am grateful. But the best gifts heaven has you earn. You buy——." His voice became curiously firm—"I think I'm afraid to pay the price."

Well, I gave up. Here was one of the cleverest youngsters on earth who threw away a fortune such as is given to few, and he was talking about earning and prices.

"You never knew the cost of anything in your life," I said, "nor how to earn it."

He almost leaped at me across the table. "That's it! That's it! I don't realize the cost and I doubt if I could earn it!"

I was through. I told him so. The lobster was tasty. They gave you plenty of melted butter with it. I didn't have to worry about the company—for they were honest plain people who ate there—and I did not have to worry about the conversation for Blue would maintain that if he felt like it, and if he didn't it would be foolish for me to undertake one. I ate. And ate. And ate.

Blue watched me steadily and I watched him as best I could. I could see his face relax its seriousness little by little. Finally he burst out laughing. "I almost love you," he said. "You are the most innocent dog-gondest glutton I ever saw in my life. I think it's your best virtue. Your others are only compromises."

"Isn't the golden mean the secret of something or other," I parried. I really didn't care. I never bothered over rules invented by philosophers for philosophers.

"Yes," he smiled. "Mediocrity."

I paid the check. Blue made no pretense at it. I'll wager he didn't have twenty cents in all the world. We moved out and up through the deserted market district, by Fanueil Hall, by the Old State House, through Newspaper Row, up over Beacon Hill, and then swung off toward Copley Square. I wanted to take the car at Park Street but he insisted on going with me for a way.

We stopped outside the subway entrance at Dartmouth and Boylston Streets. There was the usual emptiness brooding over Copley Square. One needs bands and fireworks to fill the emptiness of Copley Square at night. Blue stood with me looking over toward the gloomy pile of Trinity Church. He saw nothing, I know. He was in some other world, the abstract World of No Compromises. He certainly was a queer sort, Blue; and never queerer than at that moment: bare-headed, silent, tall, his lips moving now and then, his suit of hemp sagging on his lean frame, a trace of a wrinkle between his eyebrows. . . . I suppose he was thinking. He was always thinking. But heavens, he was serious that night!

A pretty girl passed, one of those tall slender youngsters who look like schoolgirls in Boston until they are thirty. I have a weakness for pretty girls. I watched her pass and then turned to discover if Blue had seen her. He was looking at me, smiling a little.

"Why don't you get yourself a girl?" I asked him. He didn't reply.

"Will you please tell me what you want?" I tried again.

Blue was still silent. He began to hunt through the pockets of his clothing—it had pockets—for something or other. He found it, finally. I think it was a breviary. It might have been a prayer book. He went through the pages carefully until he found a tinted religious card. It had a picture on it and a motto. He gave it to me.

Then he turned and slipped along toward the river. I watched him go. I felt sorry for him. Why, I don't know. He was much happier than I was, and had more reason to be. I saw him start across Commonwealth Avenue. I read the card. It was a line from the Curate of Ars.

"The cross is the gift God gives his friends."

It is an heroic sentiment, but just where Blue came in I couldn't see. I put it in my pocket, went downstairs, took a Newton car for home, and went to bed.

· VII ·

I happened to be in Boston early in November. The nights began to be very cold. Then, one day we had the first snow. Boston took the snow very beautifully, as it always does. I was a bit worried about Blue, and set out after breakfast to find him. The sight of the gold dome of the State House above the white trees of the Common almost made me forget what an incoherent, clique-ridden, unproductive settlement Boston is. Blue is a loyal Bostonian—in spite of his spiritual cosmopolitanism—and so I was careful, when I found him leaving his rooms, not to make any remark of my observations. Once, I did repeat to him the cynical observation of a westerner that Boston was chiefly noted nowadays for its mistakes—an observation true, I suppose, of many cities. You can imagine the flow of bizarre indignation that Blue loosed upon me.

Blue was loyal to his city. It was a fine loyalty, and a rare loyalty in America. For it was not the business-booster loyalty, but the loyalty of one who loved the sound and stir of its crowds, who loved its earth and water and walls and trees, who loved its ghosts and memories, who loved it as one loves a family home. Blue was, if ever anyone was, loyal to heaven and home. Home to him was Boston. Although, if you attacked the earth, Blue would have jumped as readily to its defense. He would have told you—as he told me once—that some centuries ago the earth was chosen as the Home of all the universe. He would have stooped down and patted the earth as one pats a pet. He would have told you that the day the earth was sanctified as Home is called Christmas, though it is celebrated now for everything but that. He would have told you—standing, probably, on a street corner, or against a fence or wall—a thousand things, one thing leading to another, and each vivid in its own way, until you were awhirl at the wonder of creation and caught your breath at the sudden strangeness of common places. Blue would probably have you down on your knees to salute, like an Indian, the earth with a kiss. Or he would have you in some nearby church thanking God for the earth. And you would do these things not as a result of any exhortation on his part, but as a sort of easy, natural consequence of having heard him talk. You knew he was absolutely right; though, the next morning—if you were like me—you would have lost much of your enthusiasm and forgotten much of what he said. And you would wonder how a man could be so unique and still be so right.

Blue looked pretty thin. I discovered a little later that he had not been eating well. Poverty in a religious order is one thing, and poverty in the slough of a gold-run city is another. Very few who take vows of poverty have to beg for their next meal or have to sleep out on park benches of bitter nights with an inner jacket of newspapers to hold off Brother Cold. Many a night Blue must have slept with the derelicts of the city in the evil-smelling "hotels" that charity provides for the down-and-outers. And many a morning he must have chopped the city's wood for a miserable breakfast. There were lines on his face I had never observed before, lines which told of the tortures of a sensitive soul. Blue had pledged himself to the service of Lady Poverty, and it was a service that called for a hero. As I walked down Beacon Hill with him that morning the snow, which had appeared so beautiful to me a few minutes before, took on something of the aspect of an enemy. I can understand the poverty that dwells in cloisters and refectories, but the poverty that strangles one at night when a relentless blizzard is piling up death in the dark slums of a great city is a poverty beyond my affection. But to such poverty Blue went like a man to his lover. He embraced it. That very morning I remarked to him about the two aspects of the snow. His worn face lighted with what I must call a sort of splendor. "All these things can serve My Lady Poverty," he said. "She is a beautiful mistress. She brings not only love but great understanding."

Our views were so completely different that I decided not to argue. Besides, it is difficult to argue with a man when he is talking in a sort of blank verse. But I was worried about Blue with his somewhat nebulous Mistress Poverty facing a winter in Boston. I suggested—timidly, I must confess—that he get himself a job as a janitor in an apartment house. Lodgings usually went with the job, I explained. Blue laughed till his eyes ran with water. "Aha!" he lifted his voice and thrust up his hand in a quick gesture, "My old friend, Mr. Compromiser."

"Your old friend, Reason," I shot back. "At any rate, your old friend Sanity."

He turned to me seriously: "Do you really believe there is so little charity left that I shall be unable to live on it?"

"I don't know how little charity is left, or how much," I explained, "but I do know they find plenty of people starved to death and frozen to death in a merry and pious city like this."

He stared at me as if to learn if I were jesting or not.

"I'm not joking," I answered his look. "If you plan to live on charity this winter in Boston, you had better choose some friend more affluent and helpful than your Lady Poverty."

I thought I had clinched my argument. But it turned out there was no argument. He had his plans all made up and he wasn't debating them with me. He was merely searching for some advance information.

We strode along for a couple of blocks, Blue with his hands in his pockets, his long legs swinging. He was hatless, as usual, with three or four black curls tossing on his forehead. Blue always struck me as being a handsome sort of youngster. Yet, I doubt if he ever commanded any particular admiration from women. He was, I suppose, too intensely interested in himself to interest, offhand, any woman. Blue was silent as we went along.

We swung toward the river. We found a sun-warmed bench down a way. Blue turned his dark eyes on me—eyes crammed with dreams and hope and steady courage. "You are a good friend of mine," he said. "I will tell you."

He told me.

Blue, it seems, had found his vocation. That was the way he put it. He was going to pledge himself to poverty and live among the poor. He would give up his attic room and lodge wherever his wandering brought him. He would live with the downtrodden and the shiftless in charitable institutions. He would sleep out on the parks and in the fields when the weather allowed it. He would live in the worst of hovels and the most repulsive of slums. He had been training for this life, he told me. He had been sleeping on the hardest of beds and on the floor. He had been eating little food and the worst kind of food. He had been chumming with outcasts for several months so that he might learn their ways and manners. Now, he said, he thought his novitiate was over. He was ready to go forth, with no name or with any name, to live with the derelicts of modern civilization and bring to them the story that they would never heed elsewhere. And that story? It was, of course, the story of Christ.

Blue's eyes shone as he talked. These brazen souls and weary souls and indifferent souls would never, he maintained, go into a church to pray or listen. They would not go into a mission establishment unless it were for food and sleep, and the preaching they received with their bed and fare they took as a sort of price they paid. They would not stop to heed a street harangue. They would suspect a minister or social worker on sight. But they would listen to him, their companion, their fellow, as they made their listless journeys or lay awake in their haphazard sleeping places.

"Already," said Blue, his voice quivering, "I have two men for converts. They have the stuff of saints, some of these poor fellows. You should see their new courage when I tell them of the providence of God."

So, on and on he went. These derelicts were ill-fits to him, not wastrels, not loafers. I can picture Blue with his fine drawn face and luminous eyes telling them of the loaves and fishes, or of the Master who wept for Lazarus and then raised him from the dead. Blue was confident that in this work lay his career. He hoped, he said, others would some day join him, others who would go into the factories and great offices and teach, as comrades, there, by character and example. They would be the Spies of God, he decided. Their unselfishness, their patience, their courage, their amiability, their fine wholesome lives would be living sermons to those who read only the newspapers and disdain the preacher. He even hoped that some day his spies would go into crafts like journalism and advertising and try to win men to a desire for truth and an affection for beauty. And such, briefly, was his great dream of a Secret Service for God.

I cannot—I do not even try to—reproduce the spirit of Blue as he told me of his plan. He talked with his usual intensity, and never did he seem more sure of himself and more right. Listening to him was like listening to some great piece of music. And never have I seen a man happier than he that day.

I was too overcome by the heroism of his vision to offer even one of the hundred practical objections that occurred to me. "Why not?" I said to myself. "Why not?" Indeed, in a sudden surge of desire for a clutch at this glorious destiny, I almost pledged myself to his plan. "Why not?" I kept saying. "Why not?" But caution came with its small whisper: "This isn't normal. Think of your old age. . . ."

Blue was watching me. He knew, I suspected, the conflict in my mind. I leaned over. I wanted to put my arm half way around his shoulders as one does to young boys. I felt sorry for this great lad alone with his magnificent vision in a world of selfishness fortressed by steel and stone. But I remembered the great prophets who were once as alone as Blue. Great prophets are, I imagine, always, even in their success, alone like Blue.

I said to Blue: "You are certainly in line for that cross you say God gives His friends."

That was all I could say.

It was three weeks before I saw Blue again.

There isn't much else to tell of him. I left him by the river that day and went in town to lunch. He didn't want any lunch. He watched me go a little sadly. I believe he expected me to join whole-heartedly with him in his project. Perhaps, he thought I would join him there and then. But I had to go along. I was hungry for one thing. And, for another, I had some business to attend to. Blue had held me spellbound by his magnificent vision. I could see, as he saw, this army of humble men going out into life, pledged to the arduous poverty of those who have no place to lay their heads, winning souls in the intimacy of comradeship, stirring souls by their hard wholesome lives, teaching souls by inexhaustible kindness and unfailing example. I understood his great project: this marvellous body of mendicants, unknown, unidentified, "Spies of God," scattered through the hypocrisy of our lives, in the mines, in the factories, in the offices, in the slums, reaching as no soap-box orator or pamphleteer or newspaper editor or pulpit preacher could, reaching the indifferent, the callous, the wayward. Truly, it was a noble vision. And I really believe Blue could have carried a great deal of it out. He was irresistible personally —when he wanted to be. He had put behind him more of life than even the extraordinary man. He was practical in achieving his own purposes. But his life wasn't the life for me. Business, I believe, is the backbone of our civilization, business regulated and run with the co-operation of science. That, I think, is my vocation. I want to make a great deal of money. I like the good things of life.

I have no calling for the sort of life Blue would wish. I feel that when I can get together some money—fifty millions, say—I can do a great deal of good with it. I told Blue this once. He looked at me in that queer way of his for several moments. Then he smiled.

"You have a rare ambition. You are very noble, indeed."

I went to New York for a couple of weeks. I was away longer than I expected. When I returned I went to Blue's lodging house on Beacon Hill. He hadn't been there for ten days. Nobody knew where he was. Nobody seemed interested.

I felt a strange remorse for my coldness to him on my last visit. I should have encouraged him more, I reproached myself. Perhaps, I said to myself, he has already gone forth to his work among the poor.

Three days later I received a note from a nurse at the Boston City Hospital saying that she had one J.

Blue as a patient, and that he had asked her to write to me.

An hour after I found the note, I was in the hospital.

I did not have to search the ward for Blue's cot. It was the center of a group: a nurse, two youngsters of about sixteen years, one on crutches, and an emaciated old man. Blue was raised slightly on the back rest. I could see as I approached what a skeleton he was of his former self. But my crowded fears of the previous hour were dispelled. He was smiling a smile that had not lost its charm in spite of the thinness of his face. He was gesticulating with his fine slender hands. Everybody was laughing with him. The ward had some twenty cots, about ten on a side, and those who could raise their heads were watching him. I imagine all who could walk were at his bedside. I don't know what he was saying to hold them so enthralled, for he stopped to greet me as I approached. I suppose he had a special way with good common people which he never showed to me. Indeed, I believe he was more at home with these people, and happier. The boy in him had a chance to play. And he and they were nearer the wordless understanding which is bred of suffering much.

He smiled up at me: "Have I bothered you? I was afraid you would worry not finding me at my lodging—"

My look stopped him. "Good heavens!" I burst out. "Of all the idiots—"

"I knew it," he interrupted, still smiling. "I knew it. You think this is some stunt of mine. And I'm crazy."

What was the use?

He thought I was going to scold him for being ill in a hospital, as if I thought his being ill were a sort of lark! What I wanted to tell him was that the sight of him was inspiration to me, and courage, and faith. I wanted to tell him that the spectacle of him alive and smiling cleansed me—as it always did—of the cynicism and skepticism that settled like dirt on my mind. Here he was, on his back, worn, thin, brave, smiling, the dream still dominant in his eyes,—and here he was hoping he had not "bothered" me.

I couldn't say anything. I took his hand, but the gesture seemed trivial, so I dropped it. His group of admirers dispersed. I was left alone with him.

Blue was weak enough. He had had a bad time of it for several weeks. It seems that soon after I left him after our last meeting he found himself a job in a lumberyard. The laborers were mostly derelicts and their boss not much better. They were a hard gang. But Blue got along amazingly well. They liked him and he liked them. In a week he had three or four comrades.

"They were great fellows," Blue explained to me, "really great fellows. I would have had them remembering their souls in no time."

I was skeptical. I said so. The typical city lumberyard gang is a tough lot and not given over to remembering—if they ever heard of—their souls. Blue was a little irritated at me.

"It is because of your attitude that they are very much what they are," he informed me. "You don't know them."

I didn't argue. Didn't Matt Talbot work in a lumberyard? And I suppose Blue, if he set about it, could have converted the lumber itself.

At any rate, Blue made great progress on his program. He sat up in bed, his eyes glowing, as he told me of his successes. He was afraid at first that these men would not take him into their confidence, that he would not get under their skins. But he had no trouble. In a week they were looking up to him, and speaking almost reverently of him when by themselves.

One of those November drizzles, cold, bleak, endless, a common feature of Boston, had wet and chilled the city. Blue had no overcoat and no rubbers or heavy shoes. But he was happy. He was getting, little by little, what he had wanted: the cross God gives His friends. No one ever went searching for it more persistently than Blue.

His sufferings and misfortunes were like successes to you and me. He had everything, but, as he would put it, he had had nothing. "Now," he almost whispered, "I am really making some progress. Pray that I can persevere—"

One of the lumberyard gang was a huge amiable Negro, Joe, who managed to get drunk late every afternoon. Blue, of course, became attached to him. Every night he saw to it that Joe reached home. He lived about four blocks from the yard. One night, during the disheartening drizzle, he was especially drunk. Blue as usual started home with him. Blue was no Hercules, by a long shot, and this nightly trip, after a gruelling day in the yard, drained his energy. But it did not drain his spirit. This night as they were crossing at Dover and Washington Streets—a particularly sordid and crazy corner—Joe reeled, slipped Blue's hold, and fell. A great limousine came shooting out of the traffic, taking advantage of a sudden gap. It was going straight for the prostrate Joe. Blue leaped, grabbed the Negro's head and shoulders, and pulled him back. The driver jammed on foot and hand brakes. The car skidded, swerved on the wet street. Blue stumbled forward. The machine struck. Joe was safe. Blue ended up in the City Hospital.

"It was really an act of God," Blue explained.

"Close enough," I agreed.

"No, I don't mean that," he returned. "I mean the whole business. The boys heard about it in the yard, and I am quite a hero—a hero for stumbling in the way of an automobile. But this will help my influence. And then what luck to be here." His eyes roamed around the ward from one human wreck to another. "They are beautiful souls, most of them. It is only in a place like this that one can learn the vast amount of human agony in the world. . . ."

"Suppose you had been killed?" I asked him.

"I think that would have been best of all. I know I am a coward to say that. But this life is so beautiful that I am afraid of it sometimes."

I asked him if he wasn't frightened of death. My question amused him. He was going to take a chance on God's mercy, he said.

"And apart from that," he smiled up at me, "why should I be afraid to do what every coward and scoundrel since the beginning of the world has done?"

So went our conversation. I learned from him with difficulty that he had been seriously hurt.

In his weakened condition, due to undernourishment as well as the accident, the physician feared pneumonia. None developed and, the nurse told me, they expected he would be able to leave in a week.

Five o'clock came and time to go. Blue waved his thin hand and forearm at me: "Please don't bother coming in again." He was smiling. What could I say?

As I left the ward, there were two visitors arriving. The nurse explained to them that it was after hours. They had just come from work, they argued. She let them in. One was a giant Negro, the other a stocky full-faced white with the nose and ears of a pug. They both were shabby in dirty working clothes and twirled worn hats nervously. They had evidently cleaned and polished up their faces. I knew, of course, whom they were going to see.

You would have thought they were about to interview a king. No yard slavedriver, no burly boss, no owner, could, I'll wager, intimidate that pair. Yet, they moved half on tiptoe up to Blue's bed. There was a gentleness, almost an awe, about their walk.

Blue's face lighted up. "Hello, Joe; Hello, Mike," I heard him call. The two shook hands awkwardly with him. Then, Mike produced a package from his coat. I couldn't see very well, but I think it was a book, probably a purchase from a Dover Street second-hand shop. It cost them, I suppose, the price of a pint of gin. They sat down.

Blue caught my eye as I loitered in the corridor. I felt embarrassed and went along out.

All that evening and night I could think of little else besides Blue. Here he was, in a hospital, weak, penniless, with a titanic program of heroism mapped out for himself, and here he was grateful for his misfortunes and enthusiastic about the future. I had admired his outline of his work: his Spies of God. I had been moved by the nobility and hardship of his plans. But I never believed he would get anywhere much with them. Yet, here he was already making progress. Here he was, happier and braver than ever because heaven had slipped him a large allotment of suffering. If that man was not a living demonstration of faith, no man was.

I had a few minutes the next afternoon and decided to drop in on Blue. I glanced into the ward from the corridor. His cot was empty.

I was surprised at this. The nurse was talking to a

tall white-faced man of about fifty. He was nodding his head sagely as she spoke. I disliked his manner immediately.

I could hear the nurse: ". . . suddenly during the night. Probably an embolus."

The tall man wrinkled his brow with great show of astuteness. "Well," the thin mouth said, "what good end can such fellows come to with their gin and bad companions. . . ."

With that, he turned on his heel and disappeared.

The nurse hesitated before she spoke to me. I caught a strange look on her face. The bottom fell out of my being.

"Not Blue?" I tried to say, but no sound came.

"That man who just went out owned the car that hit him," said the nurse.

My mind was afloat. What car? What man? Hit whom? I turned to her helplessly. I could not articulate. She understood. There was a film of moisture over her eyes. I could not hear. I read her lips:

"Yes, Blue," they said.

All this seems so long ago. It is not quite two years.

This afternoon as I write, the sunlight lies across my desk. There is some quality in it that makes me think autumn is already here. Perhaps it is the pleasant warmth it has when it rests on my hands.

For the life of me, I can't believe that Blue is dead. No more could I believe it that day in the hospital.

Why should this sunlight be so beautiful, why should people walk up and down the street, why should four robins hop in and out the tree-shade on the lawn beyond my window, why should the glory of autumn be already in the air, and still Blue be dead? Why should I be here and Blue be dead? Why should that magnificent soul with his great vocation be gone, and people like me still here, and the girl who waits on me at the German restaurant, and the three fossilized old women with whom I have, now and then, to play bridge, and Scott Jackson the wealthiest man in the state, and the conductor on the street car that just passed. . . . Why are all of us here, and not Blue?

It can't be so. No one so brave, so heroic, so glorious, so immensely above the rest of us, can leave us suddenly like that. He can't have gone,—Blue and his Spies of God. No. Say what you will. Do what you will. You can't make me believe that Blue is dead.

OTHER IMAGE BOOKS

OTHER IMAGE BOOKS

OTHER IMAGE BOOKS

OTHER IMAGE BOOKS

OTHER IMAGE BOOKS

OTHER IMAGE BOOKS

A 84 – 6